For Marie —

Celebrating and honoring your first year in college!!

Love,
DAD

STUDIES IN LITERATURE AND RELIGION

General Editor: David Jasper, Director of the Centre for the Study of Literature and Theology, University of Glasgow

Studies in Literature and Religion is a series of interdisciplinary titles, both monographs and essays, concerned with matters of literature, art and textuality within religious traditions founded upon texts and textual study. In a variety of ways they are concerned with the fundamental issues of the imagination, literary perceptions and theory, and an understanding of poetics for theology and religious studies.

Published titles

David Scott Arnold
LIMINAL READINGS: Forms of Otherness in Melville, Joyce and Murdoch

John Barbour
THE CONSCIENCE OF THE AUTOBIOGRAPHER: Ethical and Religious Dimensions of Autobiography

Frank Burch Brown
RELIGIOUS AESTHETICS: A Theological Study of Making and Meaning

Robert Detweiler
BREAKING THE FALL: Religious Readings of Contemporary Fiction

Tibor Fabiny
THE LION AND THE LAMB: Figuralism and Fulfilment in the Bible, Art and Literature

Paul S. Fiddes
FREEDOM AND LIMIT: A Dialogue between Literature and Christian Doctrine

list continued on next page

list continued from previous page

Max Harris
THEATRE AND INCARNATION

David Jasper and Colin Crowder (*editors*)
EUROPEAN LITERATURE AND THEOLOGY IN THE
TWENTIETH CENTURY: Ends of Time

David Jasper
THE STUDY OF LITERATURE AND RELIGION: An Introduction

David Jasper and R.C.D. Jasper (*editors*)
LANGUAGE AND THE WORSHIP OF THE CHURCH

Werner G. Jeanrond
THEOLOGICAL HERMENEUTICS: Development and Significance

Ann Loades and Michael McLain
HERMENEUTICS, THE BIBLE AND LITERARY CRITICISM

George Pattison
KIERKEGAARD: THE AESTHETIC AND THE RELIGIOUS

Ulrich Simon
PITY AND TERROR: Christianity and Tragedy

Series Standing Order

If you would like to receive future titles in this series as they are published, you can make use of our standing order facility. To place a standing order please contact your bookseller or, in case of difficulty, write to us at the address below with your name and address and the name of the series. Please state with which title you wish to begin your standing order. (If you live outside the United Kingdom we may not have the rights for your area, in which case we will forward your order to the publisher concerned.)

Customer Services Department, Macmillan Distribution Ltd
Houndmills, Basingstoke, Hampshire, RG21 2XS, England.

Liminal Readings

Forms of Otherness in Melville, Joyce and Murdoch

DAVID SCOTT ARNOLD
Assistant Professor of Religious Studies
Oregon State University, Corvallis

© David Scott Arnold 1993

All rights reserved. No reproduction, copy or transmission of this publication may be made without written permission.

No paragraph of this publication may be reproduced, copied or transmitted save with written permission or in accordance with the provisions of the Copyright, Designs and Patents Act 1988, or under the terms of any licence permitting limited copying issued by the Copyright Licensing Agency, 90 Tottenham Court Road, London W1P 9HE.

Any person who does any unauthorised act in relation to this publication may be liable to criminal prosecution and civil claims for damages.

First published 1993 by
THE MACMILLAN PRESS LTD
Houndmills, Basingstoke, Hampshire RG21 2XS
and London
Companies and representatives
throughout the world

ISBN 0-333-55566-X

A catalogue record for this book is available from the British Library.

Printed in Hong Kong

To Wendy
and our children
Nathan Emerson, Marie Elizabeth and Emily Michelle

Contents

General Editor's Preface	ix
Acknowledgements	x
1 The Reader's Share in the Narrative Events of Religion and Literature	1
2 Limning the Literary Universe: Coleridge, Jung and the Imagination of Otherness	9
3 Metaphysical Otherness: Reading the Wonder of Ishmael's Telling	40
4 Epiphanic Otherness: *Ulysses'* 'Eumaeus' Episode and the Ambush of the Reader's Expectations	64
5 Hermeneutic Otherness: 'A Feeling of Deflection from a Viable Centre' in Reading *A Severed Head*	87
6 Conclusion: Religion, Literature and the Ethics of Reading Narrative	117
Notes	141
Select Bibliography	157
Index	160

General Editor's Preface

Iris Murdoch wrote in 1958 that 'the story is almost as fundamental a human concept as the thing, and however much novelists may try, for reasons of fashion or art, to stop telling stories, the story is always likely to break out again in a new form'. David Scott Arnold's study takes this observation with utmost seriousness, and develops its implications within a subtle argument of literary, religious and anthropological understanding.

Beginning with a careful examination of the Western literary understanding since Plato and Aristotle, Arnold establishes a position firmly opposed to the 'isolating habits' of so much contemporary criticism. Attention is firmly focused on the 'otherness' of the text through the processes of reading and the reader's participation in the generation of the dense experience of literature.

Here is a powerful response to the solipsisms of our God-forsaken, post-modern world. In a detailed examination of three major works of fiction by Melville, Joyce and Iris Murdoch, the narrative returns us to the 'risky allegiance' to otherness, the numinous liminality of the everyday, and the disconcerting, imaginative sense of the density of our lives.

Literature, in these terms, remains open-ended, unstable, but it becomes liberalising and resists closure. Necessarily, the argument of the book concludes with an ethical discussion, for it is from a sense of the ethical responsibility of texts and reading that an imaginative religious sensitivity can return to the stuff of our ordinary, everyday lives, disrupted and shaped anew by such experience. In its careful readings and its deep understanding of major critical currents, this book will become an important and reliable guide to our reception of modern fiction and its religious implications.

DAVID JASPER

Acknowledgements

It is with heartfelt joy that I am able to thank colleagues for their abiding support, communal warmth and interest in the ideas lodged within this book, for it is they who have helped me see the nature of the way when it is made manifest in the art of teaching, in the ceaseless effort to make the classroom an apt setting for astonishment and imaginative encounter: from the years when we taught at Paul Quinn College, I thank Susann McDonald and Michael Carter; from the years at the University of North Carolina at Chapel Hill, I thank Peter Iver Kaufman, Grant Wacker, Charles Long and Gary Herion; and from the years here at Oregon State University, I thank all my colleagues in the Department of Religious Studies, but most especially Nicholas Yonker for his sympatico, humour and kinship of so many shared thoughts.

I wish also to express deep gratitude to all my students. None of my interests expressed in *Liminal Readings* could possibly have been endured without their willingness to allow me to be a fellow student, a partner in dialogue: Jenny Doctor from Paul Quinn, Sally Pont, Lamar Mitchell, Sophie Sartain and Peter Hatcher from UNC – Chapel Hill, and those who currently enrich my seminars on Dostoevsky and Virginia Woolf here at Oregon State – I feel thankfully indebted to you all.

Thanks of more than an academic sort go out to friends who, from these last few years in Oregon, have enriched my living immeasurably in matters literary and religious, especially Kay Novak, Ramona and Wayne Stover, Jean Pokorny, John Dennis and David Grube. Other friendships have endured half a lifetime, and this book probably owes as much to Jerry Keefe, Marcus Ford and Philip Lewin as to any community I have known.

I am grateful for the critical suggestions on earlier drafts of the chapters on Melville, Joyce and Murdoch offered by Clark Griffith, Richard Ellmann and Joseph Hynes. I should also like to thank the generous communities of reception at several annual meetings of the American Academy of Religion for their willingness to hear my thoughts on the possibilities of the field of literature and religion. And it is an especial pleasure to acknowledge the most recent forums for my 'trying out' of such issues, the colleagues from many countries assembled for two conferences sponsored by the Centre for the Study of Literature and Theology at the University of Durham, events organized and spurred on by the able skills of David Jasper and Terry Wright.

I would like to think that the memory of William J. Handy, Jr, is present in my 'best' moments of teaching and writing. Bill was the finest teacher of the spirit of literature I ever knew, and I wish to record my gratitude for all that he was able to show me about the power of literature and the visions it can hold out for us as we 'hurrah the harvest'. And to Robert Detweiler, whose encouragement has sustained my pursuit of the field of literature and religion in ways beyond every expectation, I conclude with deeply felt thanks.

An earlier version of Chapter 3 was first published as '"But the Draught of a Draught": Reading the Wonder of Ishmael's Telling', in *Semeia: An Experimental Journal for Biblical Criticism*, Reader Response Approaches to Biblical and Secular Texts no. 31 (Atlanta, Ga: Scholars Press, 1985). Permission to reprint this material has been kindly granted by the editor of the volume, Robert Detweiler, and by the publisher.

Grateful acknowledgement is also made for the quotation of passages from *A Severed Head* by Iris Murdoch; copyright © 1961, renewed © 1989 by Iris Murdoch; used by permission of Viking Penguin, a division of Penguin Books USA Inc., and Chatto and Windus.

1
The Reader's Share in the Narrative Events of Religion and Literature

> There will always be an Other, or the dream of otherness. Literature is the form that dream takes in an enlightened mind.[1]
>
> The limns are experienced.[2]
>
> Learning to read novels, we slowly learn to read ourselves.[3]

This study intends to undertake questions of narrative in modern literary texts by engaging the interdisciplinary field of religion and literature. In so doing, the work reflects recent developments in literary theory, especially those emanating from discussions of reader-response criticism and hermeneutics. I wish to look at certain of those works, as J. Hillis Miller recently put it, 'which disrupt the minds of their readers and shape them anew'.[4]

I have always loved stories; more recently, during my years of teaching, I have been struck by how necessary they seem to be for an adequate understanding of the liminal nature of religion. Those of us who teach in the field of religion and literature in universities find ourselves identifying with that field in no small measure because of our passion for the reading and telling of significant stories and our conviction that the communication of such passionate wonder ought not be lost on our traditional forms of academic religious discourse. What follows in this work is my effort to respond to the power of certain narrative texts that seem integral to an understanding of our liminal creaturehood, stories of 'dearest deep down' otherness that powerfully communicate who we are and how we might be better.[5] There are imaginative readings, I intend to show, which press us as readers into a liminal situation 'on the way', mindful of the memory of who we once were before the reading began, sensitive in various degrees to who we might (desire to) become, entangled creatively in an uncharted area between the formal constraints of the narrative and the creative freedom of our response, between the mirror and the lamp. Certain works of literature engage our awareness in such a dynamic way that our lives are seen to be, as Philip Wheelwright remarks, 'always on the borderland of a something more'.[6] The 'threshold of otherness' detailed by Wheelwright may take innumerable imaginative forms, and in the present volume I wish to describe three: the metaphysical, the epiphanic and the hermeneutical. Through reading we confront the Other, the not-self, so shaped that our imagination, as Murdoch would have it, may become ethically limned. Such a process may involve a reconceiving of the province of the imagination as it was presented by Coleridge a century ago, and so this is where my discussion begins, in Chapter 2. Once the reader's encounter with the forms of otherness offered by Melville, Joyce and Murdoch has been discussed, I shall return again to the ethical dimension of reading in Chapter 6.[7]

Each of this book's three chapters of applied criticism (Chapters 3–5) holds to some measure of self-sufficiency, yet all lean to the common preoccupation with the experience of reading fictional narrative, and all admit there to be a certain kind of pressure on the reader which deserves a certain kind of articulation. Wayne Booth presently remarks the degree of readerly openness necessary for such narrative pressure: 'we discover the powers of any narrative only in an act of surrender. Reference to the depth, force, and quality of that surrender is our initial indispensable resource as we then compare it with other invitations from other narratives.'[8] As the reader appropriates the otherness of the text being read, lineaments of meaning are spun. This book intends to be a celebration of such spinning, and attempts, as Ishmael would urge, to be social with the shuttle.

I am concerned, certainly, with possible 'meanings' of the novels under consideration, but just as certainly I am interested in the process, the strategy, which the reader goes about employing in getting to understand them. The thrust, of course, is that the process is part of the meaning. In all the works considered, narrative method seems to me to be part of their very substance, expressive of what, in the deepest sense, these narratives are about. All the works I have chosen are notorious in some measure for their ways of leading the reader into the joys of reading a fascinating story 'for the plot', and into ambiguity and away from the purchase of a single 'meaning'. Each of these fictions forces the reader into a constructive role, because each of these texts offers, in the words of Edward Said, 'an invitation to unforeseen estrangements from the habitual'.[9] Most of the critical works informing my discussions may be characterised by the degree to which they recognise ambiguity and by the way they come to terms with it.

Each chapter of practical criticism takes characterisation and rereading to be fundamental for critical discussion, and each (following the lead of the theoretical discussion contained below in the second chapter) intends consciously to show ways of understanding the literary work beyond the constraints of formalism while not forfeiting New Critical insights. Each of the readings will be characterised by my own interpretative strategy of 'principled eclecticism', and so necessarily – I would have it no other way – reflects my personal experience of rereading these great or recent literary works. This is, I suppose, a variant of the posture called for by Peter Berger in *The Heretical Imperative* when he urges 'an attitude of faithfulness to one's own experience'.[10] With less subtlety, one may suggest that such a strategy does little violence to the texts under scrutiny. The structure of my discussions will not be arbitrary but will reflect the actual experience of reading, and I hope that this feeling of active involvement with literary response is conveyed to *my* reader, instead of the 'windless closure of the formalisms'[11] rightly rejected by Fredric Jameson.

Thus, this work is to be stimulated by three interpretative tacks, thematically connoted by the terms metaphysical, epiphanic and hermeneutical, brought to bear respectively on three works: *Moby-Dick*, *Ulysses* and *A Severed Head*. What I would hope to accomplish is – borrowing here a term from Victor Turner – to 'dereify' the autotelic view of the literary work by focusing on ways a character's, author's or reader's encounter with the otherness of the text is experienced by the reader.

This project will be performed in three sequential chapters following the next chapter's preparatory discussion of literary-critical theory. In Chapter 3, interpretation of the first text, *Moby-Dick*, will be governed with an emphasis on character by way of the thematic of the metaphysical (namely, Ishmael's metaphysical telling). In Chapter 4, the second text, *Ulysses*, will be explored by stressing the author's celebrated thematic of the epiphanic and its impact on a reading of the 'Eumaeus' episode. The third text, *A Severed Head*, discussed in Chapter 5, will focus on the dialectic interplay of character and reader (Martin Lynch-Gibbon and the reader's response) as it is measured against the declared critical programme of Iris Murdoch and a more accomplished work of hers, *The Black Prince*. Again, the second chapter will discuss understandings of literary theory which offer a backdrop to and bring to the fore my own intentions and methods of interpretation.

Perhaps a few general assumptions can help the reader anticipate the subtance of this book. Note, once again, that the final privileging of the hermeneutical over the formal is a strategy taken in order to recognise the importance of the experience of reading, of the reader's participation in the matter of meaning. In part, this means that I will dwell on the effect(s) of a text rather than on its origin, its genesis, its production. The phenomenological tone which may be felt in the hermeneutic role enjoyed by the reader – I am throughout deeply indebted to the work of Wolfgang Iser – is an explicit valuing of the subjectivity of the reader. Such a dimension is a matter of individual consciousness that I suspect ought not be dissolved ultimately into a reservoir of signs, but rather resolved into pragmatic possibilities of ethical response. It takes but a moment to note, after all, that greatest critical energy is directed towards Iris Murdoch.

How this view addresses ways of speaking meaningfully about literature is the subject of the entire book, for the overall focus is on the reader's share in the narrative events of religion and literature. For my purposes, the context of extra-textual meaning into which the literary work can most richly be placed is the archetypal shape of literature. This will allow for consideration of Carl Jung and his relationship to archetypal criticism. More importantly, it will provide an opportunity to discuss Coleridge and the constellation of important ideas that rightly continue to gravitate to his name, especially his focus on the *imagination* (one of the most provocative terms, along with allegory and organicism, to survive from Romantic literary theory) and the artist's originative participation in the making of something of ontological worth. Sallie McFague noted several years ago that just this focus has been most characteristic of the history of religion and literature scholarship. From Jung's cosmological archetype and Jung's relevance for Stanley Romaine Hopper's contribution to religion and literature, one may move quite naturally to Northrop Frye's cartography of the literary universe and the 'social validity of symbols',[12] a famous, ambitious project unimaginable apart from the foregoing work of Jung and other myth critics.

Most relevant to the critical performance found in the remaining chapters is Chapter 6, for it will conclude the historical discussion by pointing to Wolfgang Iser and his focus on the reader's interpretative entanglement with the text. It will be noted that Iser's emphasis provides a different understanding of the literary work than those offered by the three preceding grammars of the imagination, and one quite congenial to a prominent critic in the field of religion and literature, Giles Gunn. From the outset, it will be evident that the spirit of my arguments reveals a felt harmony with the direction taken by Giles Gunn, especially in his characteristically American text, *The Interpretation of Otherness: Religion, Literature and the American Imagination*. Of all the books employed for critical support of the following discussions, Gunn's and Iser's most fully suggest my own attitude to the value of literature and its relation to religious studies.

Chapter 3, 'Metaphysical Otherness: Reading the Wonder of Ishmael's Telling', will focus on Ishmael's written telling of his story, of his marvellous, awesome dramatisation of what Paul Brodtkorb describes as 'the metaphysical isolation of otherness'.[13] My argument takes seriously the fact that Ishmael is the ironic teller of the story told, and the chapter is forever mindful that this particular teller is the Ishmael who narrates the story as the lone survivor of the tale's events. What 'orchestrations of consciousness', I ask, are being worked up wittingly by Ishmael? How might we explore the metaphysical dimensions of the otherness interpreted by Ishmael?[14] I stress the perceptive attitude of wonder, a psychological disposition which I think is crucial to Ishmael's consciousness and to the significance of the narrative he offers so powerfully to the reader. Further, my argument in part is fascinated by Ishmael, as Richard Brodhead puts it, because his 'personal flexibility as a narrator creates a plural and shifting role for us as readers'.[15]

The term James Joyce uses for the significant experience of momentary apprehensions of otherness is 'epiphany'. In a fully secular sense, it was he who, following Wordsworth, first gave literary currency in our century to this now familiar word. Broadly speaking, Chapter 4, 'Epiphanic Otherness: *Ulysses*' "Eumaeus" Episode and the Ambush of the Reader's Expectations', will be an investigation of the epiphanic dimension of the books written by Joyce.

More specifically, it may be seen as an application of the notion of epiphany as this concept is understood especially by Joyce and more generally by various critics who have found the term useful. The body of the chapter will be a discussion of the conception of epiphany as it relates to an understanding of the 'Eumaeus' episode of Joyce's *Ulysses*, an episode well-nigh universally given short shrift by his readers. Most succinctly, I shall suggest that the reader may find an epiphanic dimension dwelling within and informing the episode in its entirety. I shall enquire into the adequacy of the concept of epiphany for enhancing our understanding of the experience of literature as it is prehended by readers in this most secular of centuries. Such an inquiry is, of course, relevant to the twentieth-century development of the field of religion and literature, though little to date has been said of the reader's participation in such a dimension. In what ways does epiphany survive as a useful term in current literary critical discussions? How does it relate to the interpretations of otherness explored elsewhere in this book?

And so the first part of Chapter 4 will conclude with an understanding presently described as an epiphanic 'moment of phenomenological experience' (William Noon)[16] embodied in a work of art, a secular moment charged with immanent meaning, giving an author, character or reader for a brief time accession to 'the force, the power of any text', as Jonathan Culler says, 'even the most unabashedly mimetic', when we encounter 'those moments which exceed our ability to categorize, which collide with our interpretive codes but nevertheless seem right'.[17] This discussion will serve as a critical preface to the remainder of the chapter, a reading of the 'Eumaeus' episode proper, and a consideration of the moment when the reader beholds, as Edward Said remarks in another context, 'a kind of gift inside language'.[18]

The fifth and last chapter of practical criticism, 'Hermeneutic Otherness', intends to engage the critical relevance of hermeneutical studies of narrative as it attends to this discussion of Iris Murdoch. In it I discuss textual strategies brought to bear on two of Murdoch's fictions when the reader recognises that a reading is being offered, as Culler has phrased it, 'at the level of uncertain irony'.[19] As with the previous two discussions, at this last way of considering otherness I work from the idea of 'detour', of taking an interpretative route around the obvious or the traditional (hence, the attentive viewing of Ishmael rather than the tornadoed rage of

Ahab, or of the weary, exhausted 'Eumaeus' episode rather than, say, Molly's distinctive soliloquy or the 'Circe' episode) into the liminal, the difference being that in this chapter I enquire into the significance of this strategy itself, and in so doing offer a reflexive overview of the entire project. Such an interpretative manoeuvre has a necessary relevance for an understanding of Murdoch's intentions, her vision of the function of literature, and the implicative dimensions of the reader's experience in reading Murdochian narrative.

One way in which the field of religion and literature found historical definition and sustained enrichment was through its attention to the artist's vision of life embodied in the work of art. To read a novel with the interests of the field at heart was to be invited to consider the momentum behind the art work, the 'feeling of life' prompting the creation of the imaginative form in its unique presentation, to feel the world view embedded in the author's special, doubtless spiritual, rendering. And this view still justly informs a large portion of the field's endeavours today.

Yet I intend to move beyond this necessary inheritance of the interdiscipline. An effort will be made to express meaningfully the reader's experience of her liminal encounter from 'what is actually given in our world'[20] to 'what might be' through the otherness offered in the act of reading. Perhaps, with Melville, such readings might lead to a metaphysical apprehension of the beyond, bodied forth in terror and wonder; or maybe, with Joyce, to an affirmation of the spiritual dimension of ordinary reality unveiled, say, through the playful language of an exhausted teller, all the while coming from prior readings, going to a further horizon, following, as Ricoeur would have it, the arrow of sense ahead of us. Or perhaps, with Murdoch, such readings might lead to a beholding of the 'Good', by way of 'Murdoch's attempt to suggest the liminal position in which many people find themselves today. They are caught between... the fantasized religion of childhood and adult unbelief'.[21]

My purpose will be to show, in taking fuller account of the reader's experience of a literary work, that the resources, both historic and potential, of the ranging field of religion and literature may help us to recognise more readily connections between literature and those cultural systems of significance divided up these days as provinces of religious studies and critical theory. The advantage is an enabling, a feeling for the truth uttered so long ago by Joseph

Conrad, that a work of literature is about the business 'above all to make you see. That, and nothing else, and it is everything'; to disclose the possibilities of authentic human existence; to help us understand ways in which we are led, in the words of Giles Gunn, towards 'those symbolic forms and actions that we regard as monumental, that are accepted as decisive shapings or representations of human experience'.[22]

And so it is that we can assent to the focus of inquiry into 'the transaction between reader and word from which meaning emerges',[23] on the side less of the author to the text than of the text to the reader, and so too it is apparent, in our concurrence with Hillis Miller's avowal, that 'the most important themes of a given novel are likely to lie not in anything which is explicitly affirmed, but in significances generated by the way in which the story is told'.[24] I am interested in how forms of otherness set the reader's imagination in motion, involving him or her in 'a going out from religious beliefs and a coming back from the facts of experience',[25] and thereby enabling through the reader fresh connections among religious and literary concerns.

2

Limning the Literary Universe: Coleridge, Jung and the Imagination of Otherness

Mimesis is repossession.[1]

Contingency is destructive of fantasy and opens the way for imagination.[2]

I

I wish in this chapter to discuss the nature of imaginative experience when it invites us to consider the concerns of religious reality rendered by way of literature's angle of vision. Such discussion might help us understand why literature 'matters' so much to us, especially when seen from the reader's perspective. I heartily concur with Inge Crosman Wimmers: we *know* that novels 'are not simply verbal constructs whose illusion building we can rationally dismiss. They are experienced as events while they engage us in a particular process of world building, feeling and thinking.'[3] And such vital engagement enlists our imaginative vision powerfully. Literature, as Albert Gelpi puts it, 'epitomizes and mediates the life of consciousness, it requires us...readers...to know ourselves in searching and demanding ways, and so opens the possibility of being ourselves and of being something different and perhaps better.'[4] This ethical function of literature is being recognised frequently today (we shall see that it has been an abiding concern of Iris Murdoch throughout her career). When we find ourselves speaking of the demand made on us during the act of reading, the forms of submission, readerly resistance and encounter that illuminate 'dearest deep down' meaning of new worlds elsewhere or the numinosum of the ordinary world right before us, we then reckon with 'deeply symbiotic'[5] issues central to the identity of religion and literature. S. Bruce Kaufman remarks that 'Religion and Literature initially concentrated on the religious intimations or the belief structure undergirding poetic vision',[6] and this is why Paul Tillich figures so largely in the field's early apologetic endeavours in its American context. Kaufman goes on to say that literature functions to 'teach us something about the religious imagination, about the nature of believing, about the place of story and symbol in life'.[7] And literature can do this, I believe, when narrative art functions to recover the experience of otherness that may lure us toward that shared horizon of cultural meanings informing both religion and literature.

Now the mid-twentieth-century emergence of the field of religion and literature, on either side of the Atlantic, has been rightly characterised as a conscious appreciation of and move beyond New Criticism's methods of interpretation. Almost any text attempting a comprehensive discussion of religion and literature in American letters has found it necessary to remind the reader of this historical context. One finds Giles Gunn surveying such self-understanding in the following catholic manner:

> We need with the moderns to respect the formal, objective character of literary expression without overlooking the fact that, as the Romantics insisted, literature does in fact express something compelling our response; and we need to take with full seriousness the normative significance such expressions can have for us, as the pragmatic critics do, without forgetting that, as the neo-Aristotelians have reminded us, works of the imagination acquire such normative significance precisely because of the matter, medium, and manner in which they are expressed.[8]

A second text also illustrates the comparative depth and awareness of the field's necessary reach and proper direction in such studies:

> Going 'beyond formalism', then...need not be a relapse into expressive literary theories like Coleridge's, or affective theories like those of Sidney, Arnold, or Richards, or mimetic theories – although all of these theories have their valid points to make at times – but rather an attempt to hazard some guess about the relation between the work's language and the end towards which the language leads the reader, while not actually being that end itself.[9]

And so it is germane to the intent of my argument that we begin by offering a selective overview of various literary critical positions that have been adopted historically in the Western tradition, positions that might help us to understand the current interest in reader-response criticism, especially as it has been employed by Wolfgang Iser. Such a sketch can provide the necessary background for a presentation of Coleridge's understanding of the creative imagination (the origination of the literary universe), Carl Jung's understanding of the archetypal unconscious and its relationship to art and, lastly, Northrop Frye's design for an 'ethical criticism' based on his theory of symbol (mappings of the literary universe). I shall return to such discussion in my concluding chapter, where I shall offer comments that I think may be pertinent to the project of such a reader-response critic as Iser, particularly as such a critic come to terms with the reader's experience of a significant work of literature (receiving the literary universe).

The quotes above by Gunn and Kort reveal an American dependency on four central theories of interpretation: the mimetic, the pragmatic, the expressive and the objective. These critical perspective, and their interrelationships, play a lesser role, I think, in the English understanding of religion and literature. Throughout *The Study of Literature and Religion*, for example, David Jasper calls for a riskier, dialectical relationship between literature and religion than American scholars have been willing to grant, an open-ended interplay that does not forfeit outright the relevance of theology to the hegemony of literary and literary-critical concerns.[10] Although I empathise with Jasper's suspicion that the term 'religion' has lost critical rigour when it is not allowed to be an equal partner in its dialogue with literature, I still find it helpful to recall the arrangement noted by Gunn before, finally, showing the contribution offered by Iser and reader-response criticism generally.

The explanation of art as essentially an imitation of aspects of the universe is probably the most primitive aesthetic orientation, though it was not until Plato that it was authoritatively recorded. Plato considered the poet from the point of view of politics, not art. For him, all things must be ultimately judged by their relation to the realm of Ideas or 'forms'. Like the law-maker and the moralist, the poet is seen to be a competitor for a faithful imitation of the Ideas. The poet, because he necessarily removes the citizen of the Republic from these Ideas by way of offering a 'copy' of any humanly grasped idea of truth – this idea itself an imitation of truth – necessarily fails in his task. The poet is restricted, that is, because what he imitates is drawn from the man-locked set of appearances experienced through the senses. Plato's understanding of (and reservations about) the power of art are nicely exemplified in the following dialogue between Socrates and Glaucon, as found in Book X of Plato's *Republic*. Socrates has developed his argument about the nature of painting and what such art 'copies'. He then states:

> Now let me ask you another question: Which is the art of painting designed to be – an imitation of things as they are, or as they appear – of appearance or of reality?
> Of appearance, [Glaucon] said.
> Then the imitator is a long way off the truth, and can reproduce all things because he lightly touches on a small part of them, and that part an image. For example: A painter will paint a cobbler, carpenter, or any other artisan, though he knows nothing of their arts; and, if he is a good painter, he may deceive children or simple persons when he shows them his picture of a carpenter from a distance, and they will fancy that they are looking at a real carpenter.[11]

Though Aristotle, too, defines poetry as imitation, his employment of the term differs remarkably from Plato's, perhaps as a reply to Plato's distrust of art's naïve acceptance of appearances. For Aristotle, imitation is a term specific to the arts; thus, no rivalry follows with political activities. Aristotle writes, in the *Poetics*, that 'the standard of correctness is not the same in poetry and politics'.[12] Also, he incorporates, together with the term imitation, other distinctions in object, means and manner. In anticipation of the expresive theory so influential to religion and literature studies, it is interesting to note that Aristotle does not assign a determinative function to the poet himself. Though he is surely the efficient cause, the agent who puts the forms from natural things into art, the poet's subjective feelings, wants or faculties are not held as necessary to explain the poem's subject matter or form. It was Aristotle who first set forth systematically a discussion of genres of literature.

Historically, 'imitation' or such parallel terms as reflection, representation, counterfeit, feigning, copy or image, continued from antiquity up to the eighteenth century as an important critical term (though, in neoclassic aesthetics, it was not the most important term). I should note, too, that one finds the value of mimesis honoured in a few very recent works: dominant texts such as Gerald Graff's *Literature against Itself*, and Frank Lentricchia's *After the New Criticism*. A representative (and polemical) illustration may be found in Graff's text, and may serve to illustrate the contemporary attention given to mimesis:

> There is thus a contradiction somewhere in the anti-mimetic position. Even to call attention to the radical unintelligibility of our unreal reality is to propose a kind of *understanding* of the way things really are, and to prospose it as an objective hypothesis, not as a myth. Modern literature is no exception to the rule that writing, to be effective, has to spring from a coherent and convincing philosophy of life – or at least of that part of life with which the writer deals. There seems no getting away from the fact that literature must have an ideology – even if this ideology is one that calls all ideologies into question. The very act of denying all 'naive' realisms presupposes an objective standpoint. Such denials can only be stated in language, and language, it seems, is an incorrigible realist.... [T]he perception that reality is problematic is itself a mimetic perception, presupposing an objective distance between the observer and what he observes.[13]

An adequate contrasting view is illustrated by Ernst Cassirer, who writes in *The Philosophy of Symbolic Forms*: 'for the mythic consciousness there is no such thing as *mere* mimesis, *mere* signification'.[14] Just what it *is* that is understood to be imitated, of course, has varied greatly through the centuries. The general tendency has been to replace Aristotle's 'action' as the principle object of imitation.

By the time of the post-Renaissance critics, and obviously with the neoclassicists, art was considered to be imitation to the degree that it was instrumental towards producing effects on the audience. Thus, recalling Abrams's diagram, such criticism is oriented from the work to the audience, not primarily from the work to the universe.

Now, a criticism such as this which takes art as a means to an end, as an instrument for accomplishing something, for achieving a purpose, may be termed pragmatic, much in the manner of

Sidney's understanding of poetry. And in the largest sense, this view has been the foremost and most enduring aesthetic attitude in the Western world, and is in some ways still very much with us today.[15] Much that characterises this approach arose in the classical theory of rhetoric found in Horace.

For the majority of Renaissance critics, as for Sidney, an important aim of poetry was its moral effect: that is, it pleases and delights as a means to the ultimate end of teaching. However, from Dryden's writings to the eighteenth century, more attention was addressed to pleasure as the ultimate end, and a consequent emphasis on universal rules and maxims developed from this focus on the audience and its response. In a more practical vein, one may turn to the pragmatic criticism of Samuel Johnson, who claimed in his *Preface to Shakespeare*, 'The end of writing is to instruct; the end of poetry is to instruct by pleasing.' Stated in a baldly negative way, then, a poem is not a work of art if it fails to please.

Neoclassical theory mirrors not only a generalised view of reality, but also the resounding influence of empiricism. The epistemological assumptions displayed in the interpretative methods of Bacon, Locke and Hume were inherited in neoclassical concepts of judgement and the wit.

John Locke, for example, proposed that the human mind can initially know only through the senses. Nothing can be created *a priori* by the mind. Without first being materially affected from nature by way of human sensations, thought is not possible. Such extreme objectivity obviously limits human knowledge in the most radical way and now one goes about the business of imagining at all. With this perspective, Platonic innate ideas are not possible; that is to say, the ideal completion of natural forms can only be conceived as being a continuing process, and not as a given 'end'.

The critical point of this position is that subjective experience can only be secondary to the primary reality outside human experience. Such reductionism yields a measurable realism which, through empirical method, whittles the chaos of experience into the domesticated order of generalised laws. And (only) this is what art can present: the extracted universal truths inherently discoverable in objective nature. Fidelity to sense data will permit knowledge of that which is most real. One attempts to induce scientifically that which *is*. Concern, therefore, is not focused on some notion of what should be, since such attention would violate what is naturally possible.

Limning the Literary Universe

It is readily evident that art, in the light of the above cursory overview, must imitate nature. This is what Pope suggests through his notions of judgement and wit. Nature and art may be understood to be on the same plane for, according to Pope, the forms and qualities of art are believed to be implicit in the real world. If ancient models of art are good enough – as was the case with Homer – they should, like nature, be copied, for 'Nature and Homer, [Virgil] found, the same' and 'To copy Nature is to copy them [namely, the Ancients].'[16] Surely, standards or rules of art had developed to restrain the relativity of taste which could easily occur as imitation affected the audience.

Pope posited a concept of judgement to keep an eye on wit. It was judgement's function to control wit, wit being that extra dimension of fancy or technique, 'what was oft thought but ne'er so well expressed'.[17] Such poetic license as evidenced in the Metaphysical conceit ought no longer to be allowed, because such fantastic metaphor could transcend the empirical validity of nature. Therefore, judgement gives one a sense of the fitness of imitation: imitation of the Ancients, of established Rules and of Nature. Wit, properly controlled, can copy out ideas in the mind with an exact correspondence. The essential stricture insisted upon is that such ideas be objectively true to life.

Burke deals with the same problem inherent in Pope's writings: the problem of Judgement (or 'taste', as the eighteenth century had it). To avoid solipsistic anarchy, Burke concludes that principles of taste must be common to all people. The thrust for direction – where does one find standards for taste? – comes from Hume. Taste, Hume realised, cannot be found *in* the work of art but must refer, ultimately, to people who experience art. Difference in judgement, says Burke, is 'superficial': it is 'probably that the standard for both reason and taste is the same in all human creatures'.[18] Burke's problem is his empirically limited attempt to measure that which is affected, the subjective imagination. Taste does not differ in kind, but in (measurable) degree. It is composed of the qualities of sensibility and judgement. Writes Burke:

> The mind of man possesses a sort of creative power of its own; either in representing at pleasure the images of things in the order and manner in which they were first received by the senses, or in combining those images in a new manner, and according to a different order. This power is called imagination,

and to this belongs whatever is called wit, fancy, invention, and the like. But... the imagination is incapable of producing anything new.[19]

Note the emphasis on sensation; it is viewed as the original vehicle for the knowledge with which wit can juggle. Like Pope, Burke's concept of the wit can be a fresh expression of representative truth, but it is unique only in its recombination of the 'given', primary sense perceptions. A true power of imaginative creation, ontologically distinct in its subjective brewery, is not admitted by the neoclassicists. The reductionist attempt to do away with all uniquenesss and particularity in experience severely limits this literary theory. The goal of finding some scientifically verifiable, unchanging principle of aesthetic judgement disallows appreciation for anything of qualitative depth and spirituality present in human experience. Such blatant avoidance of subjective creativity reveals how implacable the neoclassical theory of imitation had become.

Particularly after Hobbes and Locke in the seventeenth century, attention began to be focused upon the mental constitution of the poet, the characteristics of his genius, and the engagement of his faculties in creating a poem. With this arrival of an expressive theory of art, one enters the Romantic Age, in which poetic composition, as Wordsworth expressed it famously, 'is the spontaneous overflow of power feelings'.[20] It is the artist, from this perspective, who is of central concern, for poetry is now defined in terms of the imaginative process which incorporates, changes, fuses the poet's thoughts and feelings. Rather than inquiring whether or not the poem is accurately reflective of nature, or adequate to the needs and judgements of the audience, the criterion is now formulated this way: Is the poem sincere? Is it genuine? Does it match the intention, the feeling, and the actual state of mind of the poet while composing? The poem, therefore, is no longer primarily viewed and judged as an actual or improved reflection of nature; instead, by about 1800 it is seen to be a window into the subjectivity of the poet himself.

Unlike neoclassical criticism, Romantic theories insist that genre no longer has to fit established laws or rules. It is now seen to be much more adaptable, primarily because many of the problems regarding taste as defined by the audience dissolve when the focus of the work of art centres upon the feelings of the poet himself. Aesthetic judgement is now autonomous and disinterested, with the notion of genre now viewed as poetry itself, with all the corruscations of creativity, genius and originality found in the imagination, as it is poetically expressed. Poetry is not juxtaposed to prose, but to the unemotional, feelingless attitude of science and mere factuality. Accordingly, Wordsworth believed that neoclassical theory was inadequate because its diction was not efficacious in evoking feelings. Feeling now becomes the basis of taste, and such emotive expression is not subservient to scientific verification.

Poetic figures of speech and rhythm, because they can express the genuine and spontaneous feelings of the poet, can communicate a sensitivity that is recreated in the audience. Imagery thus is regarded as valuable. The insight into reality by the poet is different from that of the audience in degree, not kind. So it naturally follows that the feelings in all humanity may be educated by way of poetry's pleasurable association with these feelings. Indeed, the notion of the uniformity of sensibility is advanced.

Thus there emerged a position which is fundamentally different from the common inheritance of the critical tradition. The expressive position stresses that the highest form of poetry is that found in the lyrical genre, that the criterion is spontaneity and that, with regard to the external world, poetry no longer needs to be true to the object, but rather to the human emotion. Again, the fate of the audience is also drastic, for it is reduced to a single member: the poet himself. As John Stuart Mill suggests, 'All poetry is of the nature of soliloquy.'[21] Pressed to its highest pitch, the grandest claim of classical romanticism is that 'the poetic imagination is the most significant thing the world had ever known'.[22]

Accordingly, as 'the long shadow of Coleridge' (Richard Macksey's phrase)[23] developed historically, difficulties became more apparent. By the time of Mill and Shelley, poetry had become identified with the inner, solitary experience of the poet. To phrase the matter with more point, actual poetry focuses on the mind working, as a *process* of the mind. Such emphasis eventually excludes any possibility of the poem remaining an object, a development that subsequently galled early twentieth-century criticism. One must also raise those purdurable questions of sincerity and sentimentality. To what degree *do* one's beliefs have to correspond to those of the poet's in order to appreciate his poetry? Just how much can one know about a poet's subjective nature, indeed? No sense of specificity in poetry remains: vagueness reigns, and it appears that genre has to be cast aside. Keeping with Shelley a moment longer, one must ask: if the poet is seen to be the legislator of the world, does not this identify feeling with morality? One need look no further than T. S. Eliot's characteristic attempt to divorce the poet's personality from the poem itself to discover one essential consequence in the history of modern literary criticism. Eliot believed that one must emphasise the objective nature of the work itself, and so the revivification of genre occurs with the concern for technique and form. Meaning then becomes that found only in the poem, and the feeling of the poem is differentiated from the feeling of the poet. This becomes a necessary component of the formalist view of art, a theory of semantic autonomy proposing that the literary work 'is a necessary and not a contingent thing'. It is a thing, W.J. Harvey recalls in his description, 'wrenched from the chaotic flux of the experienced world; it has its own laws and its own firm structure of relationships; it can, like a system of geometry, be held to be absolutely true within its own conventionally established terms'.[24] It may be seen, then, that the Romantic understanding of genre as poetry itself has few interpretative tools (and less concern) for other genre identified through the excellent use of words and how they are arranged.

An objective theory obtains when the work of art is held to be self-sufficient unto itself, when it is evaluated and understood only by its interior alignments, its interior mode of being, completely divorced from the exterior world. This critical purview continues to be very much with us today, an influence described by Lentricchia as 'a continuing urge to essentialize literary discourse by making it a unique kind of language – a vast, enclosed textual and semantic preserve'.[25] The art work is necessarily understood in isolation as an autonomous whole, and its significance and value are determined without any reference beyond itself; mimesis is banished, since it would permit access to the object of a work as anterior to the work itself (rather than claiming that the work's object and the work must be utterly coincidental). The consequences of such a view have not been lost on some of the present generation of religion and literature scholarship. In *Transfiguration*, Frank Burch Brown writes:

> if all languages are seen to be so interconnected as to be parasitical on each other without ever affording access to actualities beyond language itself, then one pays the price of removing the 'other' from discourse and thought. When this happens, one wit-

nesses the disappearance of any self, neighbor, world or God that might warrant love or care.[26]

After a sustained discussion of Coleridge as an exemplary figure of the expressive model, one who continues to offer a base for inaugurating discussions of a 'poetics of belief', we shall find ourselves returning frequently to discussions of the objective theory as it relates to Jung and the received readings of Melville and Joyce. In the concluding chapter, we shall note how it is transformed by Frye and a more recent shift in critical attention represented by reader-response critical theory. In the last section of that chapter, then, I shall focus on Wolfgang Iser as a contemporary instance of a conscious move beyond the isolating habits of mind registered by the New Criticism.

II

Coleridge wished to bring the whole soul of man into activity. Scarcely a writer or critic has doubted – in words at any rate – that literature aims to involve something approaching man's whole being.[27]

As an initial response to the above cursory overview, one might note with interest that, viewed historically, critical theories have been remarkably characterised by their particular points of departure. Much of that which may be found wanting has been brought about by the critic's inability or unwillingness to begin enquiry at any point other than embraced initially. For example, if it is seriously believed that the mind does not contribute anything creatively 'new' to what is thought to be real, no exploration into subjective experience is deemed necessary, for the mind can only 'reflect' that which is 'out there'. Hence, imitative theories of art are brought to mind. Likewise, if one understands the mind as being a constitutively formulating faculty for what can be known, one might run the risk of being solipsistic. Kant and his disciples are understood by many to define reality as that which is known solely by way of mental constructs. The 'noumenal' can only be presumed, and yet frustration about such a bifurcation in experience is apparent in Schelling, and is resisted in our century in the remarkable work of Whitehead and his process cosmology.

We have also noted the theories of didacticism, and how they append the primary definition of poetry upon ways that poetry 'affects' the audience. By contrast, early twentieth-century critical thought emphasised the objective reality of the poem itself. If one holds that the poem is the proper object of attention, then critical strategies may be fruitfully applied only to this object as a thing in and of itself. The New Criticism was predicated on the teleological unity of the literary work, for example, for a work could be viewed, in the words of Meyer Abrams, as 'a self-contained universe of which we cannot demand that it be true to nature, but only, that it be true to itself'.[28] Other criticism, such as that characteristic of Philip Wheelwright and R.P. Blackmur, recognises the need to attend to the critical act with as inclusive an attitude as possible (or, say, as the work of art will permit). One can hear in the following two quotes from David Hoy and Wheelwright both the respect for the *otherness* of the literary work and the need to make anthropological claims for the word 'meaning' that necessarily reach beyond the text to the experience of liminality:

> If we did not experience the text as other, if we experienced it as merely something of our own invention or something completely familiar (Schleiermacher), we would not be caught up by and interested in the text.[29]

> To be conscious is not just to be; it is to mean, to intend, to point beyond oneself, to testify that some kind of beyond exists, and to be ever on the verge of entering into it altough never in the state of having full entered. The existential structure of human life is radically, irreducibly *liminal*.[30]

And so one may not be satisfied to assume that a poem has 'being', that it just 'is'. Whether or not it is a violation of its 'is-ness' to admit that a poem has meaning for any inquiring sensibility it touches has been a matter of critical concern for decades. We find Culler remarking in *The Pursuit of Signs*, for instance: 'A major development in recent criticism has been the focus on the reader, both in theories of signification and in criticism that describes the meaning of the work as the experience it provokes in the reader.'[31] The readings of Melville, Joyce and Murdoch that follow are liminal because meaning is being experienced in this sense.

The mere presence of any poem may suggest that this 'object' must have been 'created' by some individual personality existing in history. For some critics, queries of whence a poem's creation are psychologically important for a more complete understanding of the full poetic experience. For a clear illustration, one may look at E.D. Hirsch. His central thesis is that meaning is determined by authorial will, that the author's intention is the determinant of textual meaning. At the opposite end of the spectrum we find Hans-George Gadamer insisting that the effect of a text is an important constituent of its meaning. It is of equal significance, that is to say, to recognise that no poem can be unless some audience at some time takes notice of and experiences the poetic object. One need not fall into the interpretative posture that I.A. Richards defined early in his career. And yet it is important to recognise that Richards was on to something: feelings and attitudes actually do exist in the poet and in the reader, and it is important to enquire about a poem's relationship to such feelings. It is just as important, of course, not to locate the poem's reality entirely within creative impulses and attitudinal responses (this latter fault may justly be levelled at David Bleich). Let us now return to Coleridge and his understanding of the imagination.

As Susanne Langer suggested in *Philosophy in a New Key*,[32] the history of ideas does not progress significantly by the collection of factual information, but rather by the quality of the questions asked. In view of this idea, let us formulate the following question (Coleridge would have believed it to be absolutely vital to his critical position): Is what one calls the imagination limited – as British empirical theory and associationist psychology of Hobbes and Hume held that it was – to the recombination of materials supplied to it by the senses, or is it capable of genuine creation? Is it able to body forth before the mind's eye what was never even in its constituent parts?

Though such a question is hypothetical, it nevertheless serves to highlight the historical relevance of much that Romantic theorists were willing to consider, for the Romantic enterprise applied an expressive interpretation to its understanding of reality. It thereby elevated the status of feelings within the self and accorded this same emphasis to the substance of poetry. Such a *Weltanschauung*, initiated through the Romantic threshold, is aptly described by Abrams in his classic, *The Mirror and the Lamp*:

A work of art is essentially the internal made external, resulting from a creative process operating under the impulse of feeling, and embodying the combined product of the poet's perceptions, thoughts, and feelings. The primary source and subject matter of a poem, therefore, are the attributes and actions of the poet's own mind; or if aspects of the external world, then these only as they are converted from fact to poetry by the feelings and operations of the poet's mind.[33]

Now, when placed within the scape of the dynamics of history, this statement suggests a general position inaugurated, developed and embraced over a period which stems in part from Immanuel Kant's revolutionary doctrine of imagination (*Einbildungskraft*): the mind is actively constitutive of the world it knows. Indeed, this doctrine, to borrow a phrase from William Wimsatt and Cleanth Brooks,[34] is 'the ghostly paradigm' which informs Coleridge's understanding of the imagination.

For the purposes of this chapter, romanticism may be seen as a 'highly self-conscious literary movement', since it was a determined response to the analytic and empirical trends of the seventeenth and eighteenth centuries. The movement was initially German, and included such critics as J.G. Herder, A.W. Schlegel, Schiller, Goethe, Hegel and Schelling. It strove to reconstruct, to revitalise a world rendered abstract and mechanical by Cartesian and Hobbesian philosophies. These German romantics also sought to regain a harmony between subject and object, between the human and nature, 'between the vital, purposeful, value-ful world of private experience and the dead postulated world of extension, quantity, and motion'[35] of scientism. Wimsatt and Brooks clearly delineate not only the link between the German movement and its English precursors, but also the real historical advance that was accomplished:

> The work of the British aestheticians, literary theorists, and writers on genius lay ready for the German transformation. The transformation, the stepping up, was nevertheless a matter of great moment. What was emprical, descendental, down-looking, matter-of-fact in the British pioneering, became with the Germans metaphysical, transcendental, ideal, and absolute. Theories of how human feelings and trains of consciousness *happen* to work became theories of what art *is*, what poetry *is*, and the *is* implied the ought to be.[36]

Limning the Literary Universe

There is a parallel, then, between this transformation's relation to mid-eighteenth-century British aesthetics and criticism and Kant's relation to Hume.

As we come now to the direct discussion of Coleridge's theory of the imagination, it would be prudent to acknowledge the remarkable degree of indebtedness of his ideas of those of the German literary movement discussed above. One of the clearest accounts of this fact is found in the second volume of Rene Wellek's *A History of Literary Criticism*:

> The general aesthetic position – the view of the relation between art and nature, the reconciliation of opposites, the whole dialectical scheme – comes from Schelling. The distinctions between symbol and allegory can be found in Schelling and Goethe, the distinction between genius and talent in Kant, the distinctions between organic and mechanical, classical and modern, statuesque and picturesque in A.W. Schlegel. Coleridge's particular use of the term 'Idea' comes from the Germans, and the way in which he links imagination with the process of cognition is also clearly derived from Fichte and Schelling.[37]

And it should be noted that such aesthetic borrowing, when included within elements of the eighteenth-century tradition of neoclassicism and British empiricism, resulted in a uniquely comprehensive attempt at a thorough systematic epistemology and metaphysics. Out of this Schellingian fund of insights Coleridge derived his aesthetics, his principles of literary and practical criticism. Out of a unique combination of contemporary German dialectics and the psychological tradition came Coleridge's revolutionary theory of mind which 'was, in fact, part of a change in the habitual way of thinking, in all areas of intellectual enterprise, which is as sharp and dramatic as any the history of ideas can show'.[38]

In order to sketch a general framework, let us begin with Coleridge's cosmology: the universe, as he viewed it, was ultimately balanced, unified, and harmonious among its particulars and universals. Significantly, he saw the cosmos as an organic whole. This whole was comprised, primarily, of a basic dualism in the phenomena of nature. This, for Coleridge, was the essential law of life: reality manifests itself, substantially, as the dialectical opposition of subject and object. Or, more accurately, one might say that reality is intelligible only when descried in the form of polar opposites.

Coleridge views the forces of life as dynamically evolving, thrusting toward greater harmony and vitality, pushing up from the inorganic to higher degrees of sentience, to the self-consciousness of man, and ultimately to the completely spiritual reality of the infinite 'I AM', God. For such an orderly system, organic growth is recognised at different levels: the natural, social, psychological, imaginative and spiritual. That which is most intensely unified is a manifestation of the highest value, the highest degree of life. At the same time, it is at its greatest degree of particularity. Organic unity allows for and promotes creative individuation. In other words, the greatest wholeness should be embodied in the particulars where their potential is most fully realised.

Coleridge seeks, in his epistemology, the reconciliation of the discursively realised polar opposites, or at least a vital equilibrium of them. He puts greatest psychological focus on the inner powers of the individual mind. The human mind strives for the reconciliation of such opposites as reason and understanding, the active and the passive, genius and talent, imitation and copy, symbol and allegory. Such importance is attached to the imagination because it has the power necessary to unify. In Chapter 7 of *Biographia Literaria*, Coleridge writes:

> There are evidently two powers at work, which relatively to each other are active and passive; and this is not possible without an intermediate faculty, which is at once both active and passive. (In philosophical language, we must denominate this intermediate faculty in all its degrees and determinations, the IMAGINATION).[39]

Two basic mental faculties are reason and understanding. Reason transcends the senses to notions of truth, of ultimate reality. It is more complete, more comprehensive than understanding. Understanding is discursive, logical, scientific and sense-oriented.

The imagination is that agent which can 'bring the whole soul of man into activity'. Unlike reason, it images the idea; unlike understanding, it idealises, rather than abstracts, from images. Richard Fogle describes, in terms of ends, the relations of these three faculties: 'The end of reason is spiritual truth, and the end of understanding is the demonstrable truth of science; and the end of imagination is the beauty of truth, by means of which truth is accessible to the spirit.'[40]

Taste is conceived to be likened to the imagination because, although innate, it conjoins the 'active and the passive powers of our nature', the subjective and the objective. Taste, as another intermediary faculty, makes possible the apprehension of beauty. The following schema will aid my discussion of several terms central to the psychological thrust of Coleridge's criticism:

ACTIVE powers	GOOD	REASON
TASTE	BEAUTIFUL	IMAGINATION
PASSIVE powers	AGREEABLE	UNDERSTANDING

Coleridge envisions the mind to be most fully activated when engaged in poetic creation, and thus his position insists, as Lentricchia notes, on 'preserving the active, conscious subject (will) as the triggering force in the poetic process, as the guide of the imaginative process'.[41] To study a work of poetry, therefore, one has to explore the fabric of the mind behind the work. He is therefore interested in the complexities of the processes of mental activity when aesthetically stimulated.

In this multi-layered cognition of reality, beauty rests between the higher concept of the good and the lower of the merely agreeable. Beauty, unlike the good and the agreeable, is immediate, 'is always intuitive', and does not affect volition. That is to say, it is not dependent on and does not engage the will. It is self-sufficient. Life, as suggested earlier in this section, could be described as unity in multeity. Coleridge defines beauty most succinctly as 'multiety in unity'. Beauty is not dependent on or independent of an external referent; it is found as a living embodiment of harmony. It 'subsists only in composition'. We ought always to keep in mind, Kathleen Wheeler notes, the degree to which so much of Coleridge's thought should be seen as interactive, relational and creative.[42]

Now, all this is important because art imitates (and not equitably) the beautiful in nature. When properly presented, this is objectified in the ideal symbol, the pure symbol; it is toward just such a presentation that beauty strives. The true symbol, therefore, perfectly reconciles matter and spirit, mind and nature. Coleridge writes of this concept in 'The Statesman's Manual':

> a Symbol... is characterized by a translucence of the Special in the Individual or of the General in the Especial or of the Universal in the General. Above all by the translucence of the Eternal through and in the Temporal. It always partakes of

the reality which it renders intelligible; and while it enunciates the whole, abides itself as a living part in the Unity of which it is the representative.[43]

Man can only hope to imitate the particulars of nature. When symbolically presented, the universal wholeness, the organic unity of life, reveals itself. Unlike copy, true imitation goes beyond the objective, superficial form of nature to general nature, universal nature; it bodies forth the living presence it is representing. The symbol, unlike mechanical allegory, embodies such true imitation, thereby distinguishing between the ideal and the actual.

Maintaining his Kantian bias, Coleridge understands poetry, like beauty, as having no end beyond itself. Unlike reason and the moral will, neither poetry nor the beautiful are transcendent, for they deal with objects of the sense. The greatest value rests in that which poetry and beauty embody, for they engage, disinterestedly and with no ulterior purpose, the highest, richest mental activity that consciousness has to offer (cf. Lentricchia's remark above). A description of this activity brings us to the heart of Coleridge's central contribution, his theory of the imagination. Its most famous formulation is found in the Chapter 13 of *Biographia Literaria*:

> The IMAGINATION then I consider either as primary, or secondary. The primary IMAGINATION I hold to be the living Power and prime Agent of all human Perception, and as a repetition in the finite mind of the eternal act of creation in the infinite I AM. The secondary imagination I consider as an echo of the former, coexisting with the conscious will, yet still as identical with the primary in the *kind* of its agency, and differing only in *degree*, and in the *mode* of its operation. It dissolves, diffuses, dissipates, in order to re-create; of where this process is rendered impossible, yet still at all events it struggles to idealize and to unify. It is esentially *vital*, even as all objects (*as* objects) are essentially fixed and dead.[44]

The psychologically oriented primary imagination is the basic, foundational conception; Kant called it the Transcendental Unity of Apperception. The secondary imagination, employing the 'conscious will', is a higher degree of the primary. It is not generically different, but a continuation, from that which is constitutive to that which is poetic. Furthermore, being poetic, it can serve as the instrument of Coleridge's criticism. From the former primordial, unconscious enterprise of comparison and selective recognition, the mind *makes*, and not merely receives, meaning through its perceptions of the phenomenal world. The imagination, then, is a creative, 'essentially vital', life-affirming faculty. 'It dissolves, diffuses, dissipates, in order to recreate.' In so doing, it echoes the creative process of God.

The will and the understanding are directed toward reality. Poetry imitates, but is not identical with, reality. In this sense, art is subordinated to nature. The formalization of art, through the secondary imagination, employs, as noted earlier, volition and consciousness. Thus, by way of 'authentic imagining'[45] (to use Philip Wheelwright's term), art reconciles object and subject, nature and man. Coleridge conceives of art as a 'mediatress between, and reconciler of, nature and man. It is, therefore, the power of humanizing nature, of infusing the thoughts and passions of man into everything which is the object of his contemplation.' Art is a 'union and reconciliation of that which is nature with that which is exclusively human'.

And yet the secondary, poetic imagination may deteriorate into fancy and whim. Coleridge continues:

> Fancy, on the contrary, has no other counters to play with, but fixites and definites. The Fancy is indeed no other than a mode of Memory emancipated from the order of time and space; while it is blended with, and modified by that empirical phenomenon of the will, which we express by the word CHOICE. But equally with the ordinary memory the fancy must receive all its materials ready made from the law of association.[46]

Fancy, though it too proceeds from initial creativity, is inferior, for it does not participate at the poetically creative level of dialectical and holistic vitality found with the secondary imagination. Rather, it is merely mechanistic, receiving 'all its materials ready made from the law of association'. Fancy, in contrast to the secondary imagination, operates according to scientific method on nature. Wellek notes that its inclusion in Coleridge's critical theory is an example of an overall eclectic attempt to embrace elements of British empiricism and associationism within a primarily idealistic framework, while keeping those elements in a subordinate role.[47]

In every facet of Coleridge's thought – from his cosmology and his epistemology to his aesthetics of poetic creation – the generative principle of the dialectical tension of 'opposite or discordant qualities' in nature cannot be overstressed. It runs thoughout his metaphysical system; it is the very 'root-principle'.[48] His version of the Great Chain of Being is organic; he defines life, in *The Theory of Life*, as 'the power which discloses itself from within as a principle of *unity* with the *many*', 'of unity in *multeity*'; it 'unites a given all into a whole that is presupposed by all its parts',[49] All reality is manifested as opposition vitally struggling for comprehensive wholeness.

Note, once again, the heavy stress placed on the reconciliation of opposites, as this time they are systematically included under the overall orderly aegis of unity, life and nature, in the well-known definition of the poet and poetry in Chapter 14 of *Biographia Literaria*:

> The poet, described in *ideal* perfection, brings the whole soul of man into activity, with the subordination of its faculties to each other, according to their relative worth and dignity. He diffuses a tone, and spirit of unity, that blends, and (as it were) *fuses*, each into each, by that synthetic and magical power, to which we have exclusively appropriated the name of imagination. This power, first put in action by the will and understanding, and retained under their irremissive, though gentle and unnoticed, control... reveals itself in the balance or reconciliation of opposite or discordant qualities: of sameness, with difference; of the general, with the concrete; the idea, with the image; the individual, with the representative; the sense of novelty and freshness, with old and familiar objects; a more than usual state of emotion, with more than usual order; judgement ever awake and steady self-possession, with enthusiasm and feeling profound or vehement; and while it blends and harmonizes the natural and the artificial, still subordinates art to nature; the manner to the matter; and our admiration of the poet to our sympathy with the poetry.[50]

Within this rich illustration of 'the balance or reconciliation' of polarities, the statement nicely reveals Coleridge's central concern for 'the seminal principle', the poetic process of creative imagination. Interest in the poet's activity prevails over the focus on the poetic object as completed fact. Thus the emphasis is 'in becoming no less than in being'.[51] The cardinal value attributed to the imagination, as has been shown, is that it is very much a 'synthetic and magical power'.

Poetry does not come about passively, as is somewhat suggested in Wordsworth's formulation of 'the spontaneous overflow of powerful feelings', but actively, under the 'irremissive, though gentle and unnoticed' reign of the conscious will and understanding. Coleridge's use of the organic metaphor emphasises the complexity of the process of growth, which is 'appropriate to art and poetry in expressing the literally inconceivable subtlety of its being and its creation, the unity and wholeness of the mind of "the poet in ideal perfection" '.[52] And it is the activity of the cohesive power of the imagination that allows the mind to grasp, harmoniously, that which is profound yet non-discursive: the organic unity of life and beauty, the subject and the object, the subordination of 'art to nature; the manner to the matter; and our admiration of the poet to our sympathy with the poetry'.

III

Jung is quite palpably right to this extent, that the primordial images are 'as much feelings as thoughts,' but that their strong feeling-tone does not by any means reduce them to the status of merely subjective occurrences. Their subjectivity has its origin somehow... beyond the confines of the individual. A genuine archetype shows itself to have a life of its own, far older and more comprehensive than ideas belonging to the individual consciousness or to the shared consciousness of particular communities.[53]

It is crucial to note that such critics as Wolfgang Iser and Giles Gunn revere the critical terms 'function' and 'experience'. A connection between the field of religion and literature and reader-response criticism may be found precisely here, in those forms of expression, used by both Gunn and Iser, which critical thought can offer to articulate this insight. My essay is an effort at pursuing such articulation when this connection is brought to bear on three quite different narratives. It is an anthropological connection that we are talking about here; Iser, as we shall see in a short while, says so explicitly, and Gunn years ago remarked that the shift from literature and theology studies to the field's more capacious self-understanding as 'religion and literature' was in no small measure a response to the increasing relevance of anthropological studies in religion, such as may be found in the work of Clifford Geertz, Robert Bellah and Victor Turner.

Although the objective position has rarely been adopted in the past, it continues to be the overwhelming position found today, at least in American scholarship. A striking projection of this assessment of its unabated hegemony may be found in a contemporary essay written by Jane Tompkins, where she declares that even deconstructionist criticism may be viewed as a species of formalism.[54] To return to what consensual ground may yet be found in critical thought, I should like to pause for a moment and discuss this common inheritance of the objectivist position, for it is from this critical approach that Carl Jung and his epigones attempt to distinguish a fruitful alternative vision of the experience of a literary work.

The primary tack taken by an 'ideal' formalist is the unrelenting insistence to advise again and again that the reader must approach a work of literature with enough humility to allow the artistic 'form' to render meaning outward to the recipient, the reader. The point to be stressed by this objective theory is that such rendered meaning can only be manifested by way of the work's *own* inner logic, its own terms of infolding irony and dislocating metaphor and interiorised symbol and so on. It is only by way of those dimensions, in other words, supportive of the underlying organic unity of the work as a whole that a satisfactory understanding can be achieved. Attention focused entirely within the body of a work of literature allows for essential knowledge of linguistic structures and the reflexive nature of words as they organically heighten the final concrete presentation.

Now, when one sets about studying 'meaning' as it is rendered solely by way of 'technique', it quickly becomes evident that it would be quite difficult, when so guided by New Critical methods of interpretation, to respond to any tugging of some embrasure of reality residing 'beyond formalism', any sense of literature's participating, indeed being immersed, in the manifold burdens of history and culture. The metaphysic implied by this perspective is accurately noted by Vernon Ruland in his capacious overview of literary criticism and religious thought, *Horizons of Criticism*. The paradigm he calls for as its replacement is quite the same as that informing the work of Wolfgang Iser, and that influences the following chapters of this essay:

> The autotelist world view presumes a space filled with innumerable self-contained monads, each governed by independent formal specifications, separate worlds occasionally colliding and interpenetrating, but communicating only in the most opaque, obscure language. Such a model is pluralistic, emphasizing a strict subject – object dichotomy, [and holds to the crucial values] of autonomy, integrity, clarity, discontinuity. I think the paradigm that must replace this is the universe of Dewey, Whitehead, and other process philosophers, an evolving dynamic flux without sharp breaks and fixed separated entities. Here an organism shapes its context and in turn is shaped by it. There is an ongoing, mutually conditioning transaction between the novelist experiencing, the novel experienced, and the critic experiencing. The literary text... has the status, then, of only a relative autonomy – better, a correlative or relational autonomy.[55]

It may appear as if I am giving short shrift to the formalist posture, and I do not intend to suggest that one ought to slight the power and rigour of such aesthetic insights as those inaugurated by the likes of T. S. Eliot, John Crowe Ransom and Cleanth Brooks. After all, if one in no way allows oneself to be informed by methods which stress that the craft of criticism is a keen and attendant focus on the concrete instances of literary form, one might very well run the risk of mucking the integrity of literature as it bodies forth a particular form of reality. This form can easily be overwhelmed by habits of mind attuned to political and cultural presuppositions. I do not think that one need lose sight of the fact that literature must somehow be met on its own ground – I do think this 'ground' cannot be known as existing as a sheerly isolable phenomenon. *Literary language is experienced as relevant because it is felt to 'to connect' with the broader contexts of culture and history.*

Because I hold the above observation to be true, I think it is necessary to consult approaches which lead one to the parameters of the art work, where relationships are descried as residing beyond the inner form – those relationships shown by Abrams's model to be located or rooted in the natural world, the creative artist's mind, the audience or, as I distinguish throughout Chapters 3 to 5 below, the reader. Such a search for a more adequate understanding of the phenomenon of the art work, in keeping with the temper of such scholarship as is witnessed by symbolic anthropology, structuralism and phenomenological hermeneutics, may lead one to such thinkers as Northrop Frye, Susanne Langer, Clifford Geertz, Hans-George Gadamer and Carl Jung. In such company one will encounter such dynamic concepts as myth, symbol and archetype as they relate to the literary experience. I now turn to a consideration of Jung and archetypal criticism.

Perhaps the most remarkable quality of Jungian concepts is their breadth of scope. Accordingly, the most striking characteristic of archetypal criticism is its interest in the broad, far-ranging sweep of the totality of human experience, personally in its witness to the content of dreams, culturally in its serious allegiance to a transcending form of reality embodied in myth, religion and art as they manifest archetypal patterns. As Jung states it in his essay 'Psychology and Literature', regarding the complexities of the human mind:

> The phenomenology of the psyche is so colorful, so variegated, in form and meaning, that we cannot possibly reflect all its riches in *one* mirror. Nor in our description of it can we ever embrace the whole, but must be content to shed light only on single parts of the total phenomenon.[56]

Basically, one comes to Jung's theories as material which later critics have received for direction in their own critical application. This is simply to say that Jung himself offered little in the way of a literary method of interpretation. For the first primary instance of the application of Jungian archetypal theory, one might consult Maud Bodkin's *Archetypal Patterns in Poetry*.[57] The material employed by Jung in, say, his essay 'Archetypes of the Collective Unconscious' is drawn from religion, myth and dream, not from literature. Elsewhere, and particularly in the essays 'On the Religion of Analytical Psychology to Poetry' and 'Psychology and Literature', he deals almost exclusively with the relationships of psychology to the artist and to the art object.

Jung's concept of the psyche (all thought, feeling and behaviour) implies an inherent wholeness of the personality as a given, which only needs the necessary time to mature. He views a human as a being that does not acquire piecemeal its essential bits to a final totality, but rather as one who must strive to augment to a richly differentiated harmony this innate omneity.

Although the psyche is understood to be comprised of three levels – consciousness, the personal unconscious and the collective unconscious – it is primarily this third level that informs the central base of archetypal critical theory. Before Jung arrived at this concept of the collective unconscious, it was widely held that both the conscious and the unconscious mind basically were environmentally determined. Jung denied this and suggested that evolution and heredity allow the inchoate patterns of the psyche (called 'blueprints'). Through the (physical) brain, the mind inherits those characteristics that determine the modes through which an individual will be able to receive experience. Man, with this view, is linked with the past – secondarily with the personal history as a child, and primarily 'somehow' (Wimsatt and Brooks's qualifier)[58] with the racial, organic evolution of mankind.

First, this means that the collective unconscious exists quite independently of an individual's personal unconscious. The collective unconscious holds primordial images pointing back to the origins of the psyche in the very primitive past (the 'grey mists') and provides for one's predispositions for experiencing and responding to the world as the human form once did ancestrally.

Archetypes might be described as the contents of the collective unconscious. The term means 'prime imprinter', and it refers to our inner dispositions and propensities as distinguished from the term archetypal, which refers to the unconscious contents and motifs arranged by the archetypes. As Aniela Jaffe suggests:

> In psychology archetypes represent the patterns of human life, the specificity of man. As they are unconscious quantities, they remain irrepresentable and hidden, but they become indirectly discernible through the arrangements they produce in our consciousness: through the analagous motifs exhibited by psychic images and through typical motifs of action in the primal situations of life.... Philosophically considered, the archetype is not the *cause* of its manifestations, but their *condition*.[59]

This is another way of saying that we have no means to get to the origins of archetypes, but must accept them as inherent structural elements of human nature. In fact, in Jung's later years, he ultimately described the real nature of the archetype in the collective unconscious as 'quasi-psychic' or 'psychoid', or, employing a more familiar term, 'metaphysical'.

It is the phenomena of myth, dream and art that are the vehicles by which archetypes manifest themselves in felt consciousness. Such phenomena are important because they embody a primary way of knowing. This way of subjective knowing may be felt as numinous, as qualitatively meaningful. So an archetypal critic, in the strict sense, is a critic who believes that when the temporal touches the permanent, the intellect, the rational mind, is not equipped to discover or shape the experience. An archetypal critic would presume that all qualitative experience illustrates this inadequacy of the intellect and the primacy of another way of knowing. Edward Edinger calls this 'subjective living meaning'.[60] And with regard to the 'essential substructure of all human reality'[61] even a biographical critic like Richard Ellmann remarks: 'only at those moments when we lose ourselves and become archetypal can poetry be made'.[62]

It may now be understood why Jung hypothesised that archetypes reside at the foundation of any art possessing deep emotive significance. He writes:

> It is therefore to be expected that the poet will turn to mythological figures in order to give suitable expression to his experience. Nothing would be more mistaken than to suppose that he is working with second-hand material. On the contrary, the primordial experience is the source of his creativeness, but it is so dark and amorphous that it requires the related mythological imagery to give it form. In itself it is wordless and imageless, for it is a vision seen 'as in a glass, darkly'. It is nothing but a tremendous intuition striving for expression.[63]

It may be noted that in this passage Jung attends to expressive and mimetic features suggested by Abrams's model of the literary work of art.

Jung, in a passage frequently quoted, speaks more thoroughly, in Kantian overtones, of the inferential quality of art as pointing back to archetypal 'psychic residua'. I think it gives important insights into Jung's position, and thus the quote is offered in full:

> The collective unconscious is not to be thought of as a self-

subsistant entity; it is no more than a potentiality handed down to us from primordial times in the specific forms of mnemonic images or inherited in the anatomical structure of the brain. There are no inborn ideas, but there are inborn possibilities of ideas that set bounds to even the boldest fantasy and keep our fantasy activity within certain categories: a priori ideas, as it were, the existence of which cannot be ascertained except from their effects. They appear only in the shaped material of art as the regulative principles that shape it; that is to say, only by inferences drawn from the finished work can we reconstruct the age-old original of the primordial image.

The primordial image, or archetype, is a figure – be it a daemon, a human being, or a process – that constantly recurs in the course of history and appears wherever creative fantasy is freely expressed. Essentially, therefore, it is a mythological figure. When we examine these figures more closely, we find that they give form to countless typical experiences of our ancestors. They are, so to speak, the psychic residua of innumerable experiences of the same type. They present a picture of psychic life in the average, divided up and projected into the manifold figures of the mythological pantheon.[64]

We can now recognise how broadly implicative Jung's position may be for our discussion. For Jung, such archetypal patterns exist as configurations in the poet's unconscious, as recurring themes in 'the course of history' (namely, world, nature, universe), as contents and motifs within 'the shaped material of art' (that is, the work itself), and as configurations presenting a 'picture of psychic life' to the reader (namely, the audience).

Indeed, of this last-mentioned resonating impact that an 'archetypal situation' has for the reader, Jung focuses particularly on that peculiar moment of emotional amplitude, the moment which, from the experience of the reader, makes all the difference:

> When an archetypal situation occurs we suddenly feel an extraordinary sense of release, as thought transported, or caught up by an overwhelming power. At such moments we are no longer individuals but the race; the voice of all mankind resounds in us. The individual man cannot use his powers to the full unless he is aided by one of those collective representations we call ideals, which releases all the hidden forces of instinct that are inaccessi-

ble to his conscious will.... The archetype here is the *participation mystique* of primitive man with the soil on which he dwells, and which contains the spirits of his ancestors.

The impact of an archetype, whether it takes the form of immediate experience or is expressed through the spoken word, stirs us because it summons up a voice that is stronger than our own....

That is the secret of great art, and of its effect upon us. The creative process, so far as we are able to follow it at all, consists in the unconscious activation of an archetypal image, and in elaborating and shaping this image into the finished work.[65]

Within the aegis of Jung's interesting insights, it may be suggested that the significant allure of art is the press upon man's imagination of the need for dialogue (engagement) with the numinous contents of the collective unconscious. I use the term 'need' advisedly, but only to suggest that which is characteristic of the human psyche. I am also speaking here of that which is religious in a psychological sense; that is, an archetypal encounter with the mystery of the psyche, an engagement likened to the *'participation mystique'*. Jung's statement that 'the spiritual adventure of our time is the exposure of human consciousness to the undefined and indefinable' could, in the way I have been arguing, be understood as articulating that which underlies a reader's experience of literature.

As will be noted in the following chapter on *Moby Dick*, it might be proposed that in our late and secular era, with the attendant (and now familiar) images of alienation and anomie frequently found manifested in modern literature, there nevertheless remains the very present residuum of the self's capacity for experiencing a transcending sense of 'otherness', some felt prehension of reality offered in wonder and awe (and, indeed, horror or terror), which thereby provides the inchoate structure for meaning. In Jungian formulation, one may admit that it 'is man who creates meaning. Yet, given a view of the world that includes the unconscious, this statement... must be complemented by its opposite: the hypothesis of a meaning subsisting in itself and independent of man.'[66]

Now, I am certainly not speaking of a kind of supra-natural reality, a metaphysically divine 'Other', totally divorced from and unrelated to our world. Rather, this sense of transcendence, as it is encountered by way of the experience of meaning in literature, points, if a spatial direction need be given, downward. In a time when traditional religious formulations struggle to obtain, the contemporary sensibility may now be open to perceive, as Stanley Romaine Hopper puts it, that 'fresh wonders shine and mystery appears precisely where we thought no *logos* lay concealed'.[67] As Giles Gunn states the matter: 'The discovery itself is of the astonishing numinousness of things as they are, of the rich liminality of "the ordinary universe".'[68]

Edinger, too, notes the import of this abiding sense of numinous otherness: 'an individual's experience of active imagination [is] a process in which the imagination and the images it throws us', or are quickened, I would add, by the reader's engagement with the literary work, 'are experienced as something separate from the ego – a "thou", or an "other" – to which the ego can relate, and with which the ego can have a dialogue'.[69] This is also the place to include Jaffe's echo of the passage by Jung cited a moment ago:

> The manifestations of the transconscious psyche and of archetypes... bring with them an aura of numinosity and are described as experiences of a religious nature. In [this realm] the numinosity emanates from the autonomy of a hidden 'operator': the archetypes there seem to be an immanent intentionality which the conscious mind experiences as a superior force, as something 'wholly other' and strange, and even as hostile.[70]

Criticism, then, cannot literally be a part of psychology. It is interesting to witness the degree to which Jung himself was aware of the limitation of psychology as a method of interpretation of a specific work of art. He insisted on not intruding into the province best reserved for the literary critic and aesthetician (and here I am speaking of the characteristic 'objective' posture discussed earlier in this section):

> Only that aspect of art which consists in the process of artistic creation can be a subject for psychological study, but not that which constitutes its essential nature. The question of what art is in itself can never be answered by the psychologist, but must be approached from the side of aesthetics.[71]

Art by its very nature is a sphere of the mind which occasions something peculiar to itself 'and can be explained only on its own terms'.[72] As with critics of many different persuasions, Jung is aware of a sense of the ontologically distinct nature of art, of art as a presentation of reality radically distinct from any other phenomenon.

Criticism can only be the skein wrapped around the life of a poem – close to, and yet not part of, the work of art itself. An act of translation can never expunge the nexus, the essense of a work of art. It is in this essence – this 'otherness' – that 'genuine mystery' and 'the real place for wonder'[73] (Frye's phrases) reside for one adopting Jung's position.

In the modern mid-century classic to which we shall turn in the last chapter, *Anatomy of Criticism*, Northrop Frye writes: 'The work of imagination presents us with a vision, not of the personal greatness of the poet, but of something impersonal and far greater: the vision of a decisive act of spiritual freedom, the vision of the recreation of man.'[74] It is with this recognition that the reader moves beyond formalism and engages the mythical phase, wherein symbols function as archetypes, and where the reader experiences 'the intimation of an invisible, existential reality behind the world of objects.'[75]

Thus, when the archetypal critic attents to and elaborates on the primordial images from (or around) which a significant work of literature has been formulated, he is exploring manifestations of unconscious, universally shared depths. Wheelwright calls such participation 'Archetypal Imagining', and describes this kind of poetic imagination as consisting 'in seeing the particular as somehow embodying and expressing a more universal significance – that is, a "higher", or "deeper" meaning than itself'.[76] And, in so doing, the archetypal critic is indebted to Jung, the modern discoverer of the collective unconscious.

Jung has often figured prominently in those discussions of critics inclined to making some effort to connect the meaning of a particular work to the broader – often archetypal – significance of the symbol systems of human experience. He has attracted favourable attention from those in religion and literature interested in such connections, and thus he is highly visible in Vernon Ruland's *Horizons of Criticism*, Lynn Ross-Bryant's *Imagination and the Life of the Spirit*, and the interpretations offered by David Miller. Jung has been a primary presence informing mid-century understandings of Melville and Joyce since, whatever *Moby-Dick* and *Ulysses* are 'about', they have at the very least resonated, so myth critics would

Limning the Literary Universe

argue, with deep patterns of mythic significance felt to transcend the work itself. The regularity of this recognition is easily seen both in specific works of literary criticism[77] and in chapters of books surveying conventional kinds of criticism.[78] The patterns of connection can be direct (Jung read and wrote about *Ulysses*, Joyce read Jung), consuming (Joseph Campbell's first effort to make personal sense of the mythical was his co-authoring of a book on Joyce's *Finnegans Wake*), influential for later critics of whatever persuasion (Maud Bodkin's *Archetypal Patterns in Poetry* immediately comes to mind), and current (Mary Annis Pratt's *Archetypal Patterns in Women's Fiction* is a fine example[79]). As will be shown in later discussions of *Moby Dick* and *Ulysses*, I myself find some of such material useful in articulating the act of reading such rich texts.

3
Metaphysical Otherness: Reading the Wonder of Ishmael's Telling

> But something in [Ishmael] is compelled, like an ancient mariner, to tell the whole long story over and over again, to those who will listen. Each telling is a new attempt to fill the emptiness left by his experience of Ahab and the whale, to fill it with meaning.[1]

> And what are you, reader, but a Loose-Fish and a Fast-fish, too?
>
> Ishmael, in *Moby Dick*

I

> The world is as it is seen. Point of view is at once a literary technique and a metaphysical principle.[2]

This chapter will focus on Ishmael's telling of his story, *Moby Dick*, of his gripping, awe-filled dramatization of what Paul Brodtkorb describes as 'the metaphysical isolation of otherness'. My argument takes seriously the fact that Ishmael is the teller of the story told, and is forever mindful that this particular teller is 'the Ishmael', as R.W.B. Lewis says, 'who tells the story after the whole of it has been completed'.[3] The ironic nature of this self-knowing narration works on the reader in such a way as to provoke the reader's participation in the matter(s) of meaning. Indeed, it is precisely this narrative entanglement with the voiced interests and questionings of the wondering Ishmael that brings into play the horizon of the reader's understanding of his or her voyage 'into the incertitude of the void'. Much attention will be directed to the perceptive attitude of wonder because it is a psychological disposition crucial to

Ishmael's consciousness and to the significance of those 'orchestrations of consciousness' he offers so powerfully to the reader.

The prescribed ways to understand *Moby Dick* are legion. This chapter intends to look into Ishmael's imagination of wonder. In my effort 'to track the antlered thoughts' set before us by Ishmael's narrative, I have hardly wished to impose an absolute interpretation upon what I judge must remain as Melville's ambiguities, in order to have them rigidly 'dragooned into a pattern'.[4] I have attempted in my discussion to call attention to sundry ways that otherness has been dramatised by Ishmael's varying point of view, and I have made an effort not to brook the distinction between Ishmael as actor in events narrated ('So strongly and metaphysically did I conceive of my situation then', he writes in the chapter titled 'The Monkey Rope') and Ishmael 'now', as teller, when he has brought all the experienced events of the whaling tale within the compass of language, when he has submitted life to the forms of art, to set the story free in the literary universe, where we readers venture to experience our own manner of 'metaphysical voyaging'. I hold fast to a remark offered by Paul Brodtkorb: *Moby Dick* 'seeks to create...a literary world of which the reader must become a part before its final reality comes into being'.[5]

It is now common knowledge – for we have before us a classic – that there is much of the quest for truth in *Moby Dick*, a forward thrust which holds out implications for the teller and for the reader. For both, this quest is experienced as a journey into something 'other', and even if that otherness is metaphysically experienced as an irreducible ambiguity or as a void, it may offer forth the experience of self-transcedence. For the reader, *Moby Dick* is a telling that on an initial level exposes the modern sensibility vividly – one might almost say viscerally – to the roiled tribulations of the emerging awareness of self as it is discovered in relation to the otherness of the cosmos. This is a crucial point that I wish to address in this chapter: Ishmael's quest for truth allows for imagining possibilities of otherness which the contemporary reader rarely confronts in a literary text, in significant measure because the strategy of the telling figures forth both the magnitude of the external, vast universe and the seeming insignificance of the solitary self. This self (referred to by Ahab in one of his less-enraged moments as 'though but a point at best') is realised initially as the lone survivor of, yet within the tale told, and consequentially, after the telling, as the reader, other than Ishmael, who is compelled self-consciously to work through the ambiguities of the story.

Ishmael's uncanny telling ultimately functions, as Richard Brodhead rightly notes, to release us readers

> even from his own heterodox and relativistic outlook, freeing us to make what sense we can of an abiding mystery. He ceases to guide us so that we can share in his own central experience, the experience of active, self-conscious seeking in the face of a world that challenges us to read it if we can.[6]

And so I shall focus on Ishmael as teller, to study the vehicle of Ishmael's complex perceptions. Hardly a disinterested narrator, Ishmael is rather one given to many moods of inquiry who, 'tormented with an everlasting itch for things remote', inductively experiences much that comes strangely his way. It is his encounter with otherness that leads to his exploration of metaphysical problems and ambiguous solutions.

Before offering discussions of Ishmael and his wondering sensibility, and of the thematic of metaphysical otherness, I first wish to offer one last comment on the impact felt by the reader of the ambiguities of the narrative itself, as if a reading of *Moby Dick* has just been performed. What might be said of this 'most audacious'[7] text, when the reader comes to recognise that it is 'so literary, so *written* a book'?[8] For one thing, the reader's entanglement with the text has been a constant wrestling with several kinds of indirection and rhetorical force, elements consistently refusing to be domesticated and always resisting comprehension. Indeed, as I shall show, there are many moments throughout the book when the reader is lured into assuming that the unfamiliar has become familiarised; moments, say, where the whale in all its particulars is felt to have been thoroughly considered; moments when the reader is seduced into feeling that the work had become fully possessed by his consciousness. The strategy of the narrative, however, makes it increasingly difficult for the reader to gain detachment from the event of reading itself, usually because the effects wrought by the shifting forms of the narrative provide an intended ambiguity. It is an ambiguity that hinders the reader from categorising or subverting the text into any preordained pattern, that prevents one from trying to make it fit into any specified form, from thinking of it in any one narrow way. Thus, at the very least, this crafted dimension of ambiguity works on us readers in such a way that we encounter, during our moments of reading, what A.N. Kaul describes as a 'largeness of meaning'.[9] The reader is left with a sense that any hope for secured meaning will be undermined. This hope for certitude is ambushed, and the gap between limited point of view (be it Ishmael's or the reader's) and the reality behind it remains permanent. This is the insight shared by Ishmael 'to anyone who will listen'.

II

Is it that by its indefiniteness it shadows forth the heartless voids and immensities of the universe, and thus stabs us from behind with the thought of annihilation, when beholding the white depths of the milky way? Or is it, that as an essence whiteness is not so much a color as the visible absence of color, and at the same time the concrete of all colors; is it for these reasons that there is such a dumb blankness, full of meaning, in a wide landscape of snows – a colorless, all-color of atheism from which we shrink? And when we consider that other theory of the natural philosophers, that all other earthly hues – every stately or lovely emblazoning – the sweet tinges of sunset skies and woods; yea, and the gilded velvets of butterflies, and the butterfly cheeks of young girls; all these are but subtle deceits, not actually inherent in substances, but only laid on from without; so that all defied Nature absolutely paints like the harlot, whose allurements cover nothing but the charnel house within; and when we proceed further, and consider that the mystical cosmetic which produces every one of her hues, the great principle of light, for ever remains white or colorless in itself, and if operating without medium upon matter, would touch all objects, even tulips and roses, with its own blank tinge – pondering all this, the palsied universe lies before us a leper; and like willful travelers in Lapland, who refuse to wear colored and coloring glasses upon their eyes, so the wretched infidel gazed himself blind at the monumental white shroud that wraps all the prospect around him. And of all these things the Albino Whale was the symbol. Wonder ye then at the fiery hunt?

'The Whiteness of the Whale', *Moby Dick*, Ch. 42

If we take the Emersonian distinction between the 'Me' and the 'not-Me' as the executive principle responsible for a work's formal coherence, we would note the problem of otherness emerging at those self-transcending moments of consciousness when the self comes into 'contact with all that lies outside the self'.[10] I suggest that these moments are given thematic point by taking note of ways in which wonder functions in the text, and that the fullest portion of *Moby Dick's* meaning emerges when we note the responses such otherness elicits from Ishmael, Ahab and the reader. One's identity emerges from the dialogical interaction between the self and all that it experiences in the context of otherness. 'We seem largely to become aware of otherness', writes Kort, 'by encountering limiters.'[11]

This situation has been addressed theologically and formulated phenomenologically, and it may be given thematic immediacy by way of a discussion of wonder as a mode of perception. A central claim of this chapter is that the signature of wonder is everywhere present in Ishmael's narrative and that, because of its irony, such wonder functions significantly in the readers' realisation of the text.

One's life may be drawn taut between moments of darksome anguish and an almost inebriating, and surely celebrative, sense of wonderment of the gift of life. Expressed theologically, one's existance may be polarised between self-transcending moments coloured by suspicions of an unmittigated Void and by those offering a sense of the unconditioned Ground of Being. To characterise ours as a secular world is in part to suggest that the winds of meaning no longer waft confidently, no longer inform that one is at home in the cosmos. It takes little effort to hear the unsettling tone behind Hannah Arendt's description of ours as an age 'where man, wherever he goes, encounters only himself'.[12] To take note of this impoverished meaning in our lives is in part to acknowledge, in Frank Kermode's words, 'the growing difficulty of access to the paradigms'.[13] The best that we can hope for, we may be told, is some apprehension of a limit situation from which we might shore up a condition imagined to be nothing more initially than the sundered remnants of a once-enjoyed contact with Being-Itself. And so the legacy left us by the moderns may be an abiding sense of deep anguish.

Although modern humans may view themselves as lodged in a one-dimensional world characterised by silence and meaningless, and although they may understand themselves as adhering to sym-

Metaphysical Otherness 45

bols of non-transcendence accordingly, their existence bespeaks an unwillingness to settle for a world stripped down to raw immanence. Just so, we find it frequently argued by modern theologians that the secular spirit seemingly ignores significant and real areas of experience. Langdon Gilkey says accordingly:

> In... areas of our ordinary experience, something strange enters, something not quite accounted for by the relativistic symbolic forms of the secular mood. A nonsecular dimension in our experience appears in the lived character of secular life, despite the fact that the forms of our modern self-understanding have no capacity for dealing with it. It has the character of ultimacy, or finality, of the unconditioned which transcends, undergirds, and even threatens our experience of the ordinary passage of things and our dealings with the entities in that passage. It is, therefore, sacred as well as ultimate, the region where value as well as existence is grounded. It is *also* because of an awareness of this dimension that our common life participates in such overwhelming negativities, that it can become demonic, filled with terrible conflict and cruelty, and life teetering always on the edge either of fanaticism or else of meaninglessness and despair.[14]

Now it is such awareness that is quite what Ishmael discovers, and the accomplished telling he offers of this experience may help us to understand why readers continue to feel *Moby Dick* to be a notably relevant literary event. Yet to explore such latent elements of the dimension of ultimacy does not presuppose that one will find God. These searching of the transcendent might reveal a yawning, abysmal Void, and leave one with an abiding sense of despair. But the point being made here is that some dimension of that which resides beyond the self will be experienced, and it may be given some form in language. Such a point relates, in several ways, to Ishmael's disinherited sensibility. Again and again, as an exile he confronts himself with the meaning of his quest for possibilities of transcending truth, portents of metaphysical meaning in a world of shattered significance, a world seemingly devoid of symbolised centredness on land, a world where nothing ultimately coheres, where silence visits as the lasting response to Father Mapple's sermon.

Just as one may feel a 'felt tone of anxiety' at having confronted the deep emptiness of a 'heartless Void', so too one might also discover an opening-up of the positive creativeness of this ultimate, transcending dimension of human experience. Ishmael offers a rich image of such a discovery in one of his most extraordinary chapters, 'The Grand Armada', when the *Pequod* enters 'that enchanted calm' of inner 'concentric circles' of whales, 'eight or ten in each, swiftly going round and round', and he beholds the following:

> But far beneath this wondrous world upon the surface, another and still stranger world met our eyes as we gazed over the side. For, suspended in those watery vaults, floated the forms of the nursing mothers of the whales, and those that by their enormous girth seemed shortly to become mothers. The lake, as I have hinted, was to a considerable depth exceedingly transparent; and as human infants while suckling will calmly and fixedly gaze away from the breast as if leading two different lives at the time; and while yet drawing moral nourishment, be still spiritually feasting, upon some unearthly reminiscence; – even so did the young of these whales seem looking up towards us, but not at us, as if we were but a bit of Gulf-weed in their new-born sight.... And thus, though surrounded by circle upon circle of consternations and affrights, did these inscrutable creatures at the centre freely and fearlessly indulge in all peaceful concernments; yea, serenely revelled in dalliance and delight.

Thus entranced, Ishmael reflects on his response: 'But even so, amid the tornadoed Atlantic of my being, do I myself still for ever centrally disport in mute calm; and while ponderous planets of unwaning woe revolve round me, deep down and deep inland there I still bathe me in eternal mildness of joy.'

Even in the angularities of life one might begin to sense with wonder and awe the sheer giveness of being itself; however tacitly, one might yet hold out a sense that, in Gunn's description, the '"traces", the "residues", the "Presence" is there'.[15] Gilkey summarily states: 'Every level of our life is related to its ultimate ground; and so each level feels both the wonder, beauty, meaning, and joy of existence as it comes to us from transcendence, and the terror and emptiness of an ultimate Void.'[16]

Wonder and terror – there you have it: two juxtaposing yet powerfully felt experiences of depth that provide for an ontological dimension to the otherness encountered by the self. From what has been suggested thus far, it might be assumed that this framework of ultimacy appears directly in the awareness of dread, of an unconditioned Void, and subsequently – indirectly – in rapture, in the joyful wonder that somehow is experienced despite the world's contingency and relativity.

Yet the reader's expectations are jarred at just this level of reading: wonder most often functions in precisely the opposite manner in *Mody Dick*. Ishmael experiences wonder in just about everything that presents itself throughout the voyage of the *Pequod*, to be sure. It is surely his unquenching activity for wondering that allows him to enter the metaphysical dimensions of his quest. As the world Ishmael encounters becomes more and more symbolically imbued, corresponding corruscations of wonder abound. But such wonder often never follows; rather, it precedes and is finally conjoined with horror. Alas! What appears full of wonder is suspected to radiate from the depths of the 'palsied universe' full of 'subtle deceits' and meaninglessness. It is the 'graceful flexion of the motions' (ch. 86, 'The Tail') of this gripping metaphysical realisation that provides *Moby Dick* with much of its power. Let us turn now to an exploration of Ishmael's wondrous telling: a discussion of Ishmael's character, of what he seeks, of his metaphysical sensibility, and of his world, a universe lying beyond the self where otherness bodies forth horror, perhaps more than wonder, as supremely reigning, where the self beholds what Daniel Hoffman once described as the 'ever-present possibility of cosmic nothingness'.[17]

III

> It was a sight full of quick wonder and awe! The vast swells of the omnipotent sea; the surging, hollow roar they made, as they rolled along the eight gunwales, like gigantic bowls in a boundless bowling-green; the brief suspended agony of the boat, as it would tilt for an instant on the knife-like edge of the sharper waves, that almost seemed threatening to cut it into two... all these with the cries of the headsmen and harpooneers, and the shuddering gasps of the oarsmen, with the wondrous sight of the ivory Pequod bearing down upon her boats with outstretched sails, like a wild hen after her screaming brood; – all this was thrilling.
>
> 'The First Lowering', *Moby Dick*, ch. 48

Ishmael must have an audience that will give a particular kind of credence to his marvellous illusions, an audience retrained in the difficult balance of wonder and skepticism.[18]

As we noted above, *Moby Dick* freely makes use of conventional religious themes, but there is a certain and unsettling consciousness telling the story and devising a 'careful disorderliness' as the 'true method' adequate to this 'enterprise' (ch. 82, 'The Honor and Glory of Whaling'). Somewhere behind the screen of theme sounds a voice that never allows the reader to remain too assured about any stated meaning, and this is the voice of Ishmael. Ishmael is the voice and consciousness of *Moby Dick*. Ishmael's own horizon of understanding provides the frame in which the story is constructed. More than this, the reader is invited into the story, into a world calling for his participation by stimulating his need for interpretation. Ishmael draws the reader first-hand into a telling of his reading of a metaphysical journey suffered 'some years ago', a telling provisioned by his lone survival of the events narrated:

Call me Ishmael. Some years ago – never mind how long precisely – having little or no money in my purse, and nothing particular to interest me on shore, I thought I would sail about a little and see the watery part of the world. It is a way I have of driving off the spleen, and regulating the circulation. Whenever I find myself growing grim about the mouth; whenever it is a damp, drizzly November in my soul; whenever I find myself involuntarily pausing before coffin warehouses, and bringing up the rear of every funeral I meet; and especially whenever my hypos get such an upper hand of me, that it requries a strong moral principle to prevent me from deliberately stepping into the street, and methodically knocking people's hats off – then, I account it high time to get to sea, as soon as possible. ('Loomings', ch. 1)

From this famous passage, the first paragraph of the novel's first formal chapter, the reader is invoked to note that Ishmael is to be the narrator. Both the book and the quest for Moby Dick begin from his point of view. We ought not to slight this necessary fact for, as Edgar Dryden reminds us, 'the world is as it is seen. Point of view is at once a literary technique and a metaphysical principle.'[19] Further, Ishmael's rendering of this tale functions to involve the reader as accomplice, as co-creator, and such involvement implicates the reader with the very first utterance in this first of 135 chapters: the reader is enjoined to 'call' this teller 'Ishmael'. We shall be led, because of this involvement in our reading, to an earned apprehension of the plural significances and ciphered ambiguities of the universe. What the reader discovers through his or her experience of *Moby Dick* is a recovery of the significance of the individual act of apprehension. And yet such implicative gaps urging the creative participation of the reader vary in intensity, and may be felt to diminish considerably as Ahab assumes the centre of the dramatic stage.

At least through the first quarter of the novel, Ishmael remains the protagonist. With 'a damp, drizzly November in my soul' (what one critic has called Ishmael's 'original disobedience'[20]), it is immediately apparent that Ishmael is not at fullest harmony with either himself or the land. The illimitable sea appeals strongly to his nature: 'meditation and water are wedded forever'. What he sees in water is an image of the 'ungraspable phantom of life; and this is the key to it all'. In the same chapter Ishmael offers a presentiment of Moby Dick, again using the word 'phantom':

[T]he whaling voyage was welcome; the great flood-gates of the wonder-world swung open, and in the wild conceits that swayed me to my purpose, two and two there floated into my inmost soul, endless processions of the whale, and, mid most of them all, one grand hooded phantom, like a snow hill in the air.

Thus begins a metaphysical quest limned by Ishmael for the reader's participation into the 'wonder-world' for 'the key to it all'.

Dissatisfied with life on land or no, we realise that Ishmael's malaise is of a kind that none the less allows him to be alive to his surroundings. This is so even before he sets sail on the *Pequod*. In Chapter 3, 'The Spouter Inn', while exploring the room in which he will sleep until the onset of the voyage, Ishmael relates: 'But what is this on the chest? I took it up, and held it close to the light, and felt it, and smelt it, and tried every way to arrive at some satisfactory conclusion concerning it.' After putting down the jacket, Ishmael meditates about his strange roommate, Queequeg:

I sat down on the side of the bed, and commenced thinking about this head-peddling harpooner, and his door mat. After thinking some time on the bed-side, I got up and took off my monkey jacket, and then stood in the middle of the room thinking. I then took off my coat, and thought a little more in my shirt sleeves.

It is, then, readily apparent that Ishmael is a most inquisitive fellow. Prefigured by the 'sub-sub librarian', he is a problem-solver, naturally given to thinking and reflecting. If something is unclear, all observations focus entirely on the problem until it is puzzled out. We read, for example, 'my sensations were strange. Let me try to explain them'. Just as characteristic is his way of engaging his reader with a volley of questions: Why is almost every robust healthy boy with a robust healthy soul in him, at some time or other crazy to go to sea? Why upon your first voyage as a passenger, did you yourself feel such a mystical vibration, when first told that you and your ship were now out of sight of land? Thus, this Ishmael has a philosophical bent, but it must be noted that all his ruminations stem from the concreteness of that to which he is present. This feature of Ishmael's personality is characteristic of an attitude of appropriating reality evident in much nineteenth-century American literature, an attitude explored in great detail in Tony Tanner's fascinating study, *The Reign of Wonder: Naivety and Reality in American Literature*.

Tanner points out that the myth of wonder provided a 'key strategy' for American writers. One who wonders has the ability to see with 'the naive vision, the innocent eye' the world in all its concrete particularities:

> You can 'wonder *at*' – and you can also 'wonder *about*'. As well as the attitude of awed and reverant openness, there is the habit of speculation: the word connotes both, and clearly one activity can easily give way to the other. There is a small but significant shift from a passive to an active mode, the idea of uninterrupted sensory reception giving way to the energized imagination which adds and provides out of its own stirring abundance.[21]

It would be helpful to dwell a bit longer on this 'wondering attitude', for it points directly to the nature of Ishmael's mind, as well as to the genius of Melville's technique. Ishmael, especially in the first chapters, must solicit his reader's attention to an understanding of his method of interpretation of reality, 'else all these chapters might be for naught'. The meanings of the world are generated through acts of wondering, of 'looking'. Ishmael 'aims to tantalize',

Metaphysical Otherness

writes A. Robert Lee. 'Ishmael's itch surely becomes the reader's. Who would not be called to forbidden seas, barbary, things remote? [The] reader's physical appetite is aroused; as is his imaginative need for beyondness, for journeying across watery space.'[22]

And so Ishmael brings with him on to the *Pequod* a sensibility of radical openness to experience. Tanner views this disposition as characteristic of the American 'paratactical vision', whereby a sense of wonderment or awe receives a sense of things without pre-judgement. American writers, he argues, were searching for a new vision that would allow literature to give form to and evoke the new feelings experienced on a new, un-European continent. This childlike, innocent eye was intended to render concrete details with 'dazzling freshness and vivid clarity, richly appreciative of the wonder of creation and not at all prompted to embark on any disruptive intellectual inquiry'.[23] Thus the 'tremendous hunger to discover a new access to reality, a new habit of wonder'. One therefore finds stress placed on the vernacular as opposed to highly refined speech, in order that words might exude a unique, and hopefully adequate, wisdom which could be seen to grasp a 'palpable, proximate reality'. Just so, the veritable concrete realities of Ishmael's world can render fresh apprehensions of the radical depth and mysteriousness of experience by way of his imagination.

Now, before settling down to dealing with the 'symbolic meanings' inherent in the white whale, the *Peqoud* or Ahab, the reader must admit the crucial fact that Moby Dick is not a concept but a real whale, one of the species which is described historically in page after page of often erudite, sometimes fanciful, cetology; that Ahab, in like manner, is the captain of the *Pequod*, that he has been badly maimed by Moby Dick, and so forth. Ishmael realises that 'dissect him how I may, I but go skin deep', as he wonders about the whale, and this leads him to express both his frustration and his bafflement. And Ishmael intends such puzzlement to be ours, an effect brought about by such 'detailed accounts'. We should be mindful that Ishmael exposes the reader to entire chapters that, in and of themselves, offer a vision of reality where the whale is nothing more than 'a meat pie, nearly one hundred feet long' ('The Whale as a Dish', ch. 65), presentations fully grounded in solid, physical, tactile reality, wherein the natural order of things does not 'give off sparks far beyond themselves'.[24] At these moments, the world is solid-seeming, the world is physical and ordinary and everyday, a 'world whose hard surface seems to be all that there is'.²⁵

But of course the reader is seized by other presentations, where he or she experiences, together with Ishmael, how concrete images, placed in a rich atmosphere, add on to one another, and grow to the point whereby meaning transcends mere 'factuality' and enters the realm of the symbolic. This is one manner in which, as Charles Feidelson suggests, '*Moby-Dick* is a developing meaning'²⁶ Ishmael's sensibility is expressed in a manner directly functional to his thematic intentions by way of his capability for experiencing an astonishing range of emotions. All experience, we learn, is multiple for Ishmael: reality can never be reduced to something more primary than 'two and two'. Nothing on this voyage will be discovered to exist without its opposite. Life is depicted, at its most equipollent, as 'calms crossed by storms, a storm for every calm'.

I have emphasised above that although the self may experience the concreteness of the world with a wondering disposition, it does not necessarily follow that celebration of life is forthcoming. Ishmael realises this lack of assurance all too soon. And yet, this much must be allowed: it is through the experience of wonder that Ishmael's metaphysic is presented to the reader. This experience manifests itself by way of two characteristics: the transcending awareness of an ultimate Void (the absence or disappearance of God), and the Faustian possibility of affirming an ultimate truth precisely by way of a quest for such truth. I now turn to a further discussion of Ishmael's quest.

IV

> I wonder, Flask, whether the world is anchored anywhere.
> Stubb, in *Moby Dick*, Chapter 11

Chapter 23, 'The Lee Shore', presents a clear expression of the sea as that toward which one journeys to seek the 'highest truth'. Although he is speaking of Bulkington, Ishmael in this chapter works his way toward revealing his strong discontent with the land and his existential need to 'be' at sea:

> When on that shivering winter's night, the *Pequod* thrust her vindictive bows into the cold malicious waves, who should I see

standing at her helm but Bulkington! I looked with sympathetic awe and fearfulness upon the man, who in mid-winter just landed from a four-year's dangerous voyage, could so unrestingly push off again for still another tempestuous term. The land seemed scorching to his feet. Wonderfullest things are ever the unmentionable; deep memories yield no epitaphs; this six-inch chapter is the stoneless grave of Bulkington. Let me say only that it fared with him as with the storm-tossed ship, that miserably drives along the leeward land. The port would fain give succor; the port is pitiful; in the port is safety, comfort, hearthstone, supper, warm blankets, friends, all that's kind to our mortalities. But in that gale, the port, the land, is that ship's direst jeopardy; she must fly all hospitality; one touch of land, though it but graze the keel, would make her shudder through and through. With all her might she crowds all sail off shore; in so doing, fights 'gainst the very winds that would blow her homeward; seeks all the lashed sea's landlessness again; for refuge's sake forlornly rushing into peril; her only friend her bitterest foe!

But as in landlessness alone resides the highest truth, shoreless, indefinite as God – so, better is it to perish in that howling infinite, than be ingloriously dashed upon the lee, even if that were safety! For worm-like, then, oh! who would craven crawl to land! Terrors of the terrible! is all this agony so vain? Take heart, take heart, Bulkington! Bear thee grimly, demigod! Up from the spray of thy ocean-perishing – straight up, leaps thy apotheosis!

In the souls of both Bulkington and Ishmael is the awareness that the truth sought is not finite, but infinite in the sense of being absolute, and to this metaphysical awareness Ishmael is driven beyond himself in his quest for an answer to the riddle of the universe. The paradox is evident: as long as we stand on the shore we cannot behold the phantom, but we risk destruction once we voyage out into 'that howling infinite'. We have here a truth 'which can be verified only through participation – the truth that discovers the limits of reality through going out to encounter them'.[27]

Ishmael, readily identifying himself as one of 'us hunters of whales', knows that truth can be sought only by 'going a-whaling yourself' – only by placing oneself in the imbroglio of 'landlessness'. Like Bulkington, Ishmael's world can only be 'a ship on the passage out'. The most ultimate of realities to Ishmael, as he thrusts himself into the 'howling infinite' sea, is the *experience* of encountering a whale. He is compelled to return again and again to the religious quest felt most fully only in the theatre that yields the 'interlinked terrors and wonders of God.' He has set himself on a search for the ultimate truth with a driving attempt to comprehend the mystery of existence, to 'grasp the ungraspable phantom of life', to read the pattern of the loom.

Ishmael is often able to limn the dimensions of what he is coming against during this metaphysical voyage. The reader senses such awareness, for example, in his portraitures of two shipmates, Starbuck and Flask. First, Starbuck, the indomitably Christian chief mate of the *Pequod* who, one suspects, somehow senses the twilight of the Christian God:

> Uncommonly conscientious for a seaman, and embued with a deep natural reverence, the wild watery loneliness of his life did therefore strongly incline him to superstition, but to that sort of superstition, which in some organizations seems rather to spring, somehow, from intelligence than from ignorance. Outward portents and inward presentiments were his.... But it was not in reasonable nature that a man so organized, and with such terrible experiences and remembrances as he had; it was not in nature that these things should fail in latently engendering an element in him, which, under suitable circumstances, would break out from its confinement, and burn all his courage up. And brave as he might be, it was that sort of bravery chiefly, visible in some intrepid men, which, while generally abiding firm in the conflict with seas, or winds, or the world, yet cannot withstand those more terrific, because more spiritual terrors, which sometimes menace you from the concentrating brow of an enraged and mighty man.   ('Knights and Squires', ch. 26)

The reader witnesses here that Ishmael is aware not only of the 'ordinary irrational', but of a deeper dimension, one imbued with the spiritual horrors that one has when open to the the ructions of life, as Ishmael must confront in his struggle for meaning informed by such experience.

We note Ishmael's manifest sensibility again in another passage, where it is bodied forth in his disparaging comments regarding Flask. Such details as are here offered derive precisely from the fact that whales, for Flask, are merely things to be killed:

Metaphysical Otherness 55

> A short, stout, ruddy young fellow, very pugnacious concerning whales, who somehow seemed to think that the great Leviathans had personally and hereditarily affronted him; and therefore it was a sort of point of honor with him, to destroy them whenever encountered. So utterly lost was he to all sense of reverence for the many marvels of their majestic bulk and mystic ways; and so dead to anything like an apprehension of any possible danger from encountering them; that in his poor opinion, the wondrous whale was but a species of magnified mouse, or at least water-rat, requiring only a little circumvention and some small application of time and trouble in order to kill and boil. [Thus, he had an] ignorant, unconscious fearlessness. ('Knights and Squires', ch. 27)

It is evident to the reader that Ishmael is fully present to a growing aura about whales. To him they dawn upon his consciousness as marvellous, mystical, dangerous and wondrous – all qualities of the transcendent, qualities finally concretely focused on the Leviathan, 'this ante-mosaic, unsourced existence' symbolising for Ishmael the problem of universal reality.

V

> Ahab reduces Moby Dick to an analogy of his mad idea of nature, making inscrutable blankness a mask of universal malice. Ishmael, though suspecting a fearful contingency, suspects nature to be at base a hollow sham, hiding absolutely nothing.[28]

> The sailor Ishmael, who feels the strong pull of this 'quenchless feud', is countered by the retrospective narrator, who can see through Ahab's maneuvers as 'more or less paltry at base'.... [As] a character Ahab still exerts his enchantment on Ishmael, and only a heroic effort can capture his nearly ineffable nature.... What *shall be* grand – the task for author Ishmael thus parallels the one for sailor Ishmael: to read, and to write, Ahab.[29]

Both Ishmael and Ahab are driven to know the truth. Both are exiles, therefore, from the land and sojourners on a sea that functions as 'the locale of man's ontological condition'.[30] And yet only Ishmael can work through to an acceptance of such an identity and live without being a solipsistic rebel like Ahab. Ishmael's is a 'saving skepticism'.[31] Ahab, that moral tyrant, I would argue, has fixed the significance of those things he would know, for all that comes within his purview are secured with determinate meaning. As William Hamilton perfectly expresses it, 'Ahab's sea has no narrative development'.[32] For Ahab, there lies the certain rigid pattern of his destiny: 'This whole act's immutably decreed...I am the Fates' lieutenant' he memorably declares. Ahab finally does not submit to transformation. Contrariwise, Ishmael, rejecting determined closure, is flexive, fluidly willing to be open to the process of perceiving experience this way and then that, and then both, refusing to unify that which essentially cannot be joined.

Submitting fully to Promethean desires, Ahab is possessed with such blinding, disproportioned vengeance against Moby Dick that all possibility for dialogue with existence is lost. He personalises everything that could possibly be evil. As Richard Chase remarks:

> In Ahab the reason and the aesthetic sense pull apart. He has his humanities, as we are told.... [But] gradually his intellect is drawn apart from whatever might nourish, harmonize, and symbolize it, and in its isolation, it grows willful, obsessive, and finally suicidal. Except for the narcissism that makes a mad allegorist of Ahab, he is blind to all the imaginative versions of reality that his own mind or that of others may offer him.[33]

As Ahab, reflecting his obdurate mind, says of himself: 'I'm demoniac, I am madness maddened!' And he remains that way, unrepentant to the last (with one dramatic exception), as Moby Dick pulls him down. This motif of narcissism has been evident in most critical considerations of Ahab. The following statement by Friedman, for example, nicely points to the essential difference between Ishmael and Ahab, particularly with respect to the capacity Ishmael has for bringing a sense of self to the confrontation of the surrounding evil:

> Ishmael's narcissism lies not in contemplating his own mirrored image but the image of life and the world, and if he is as likely to drown as Narcissus, it is not from reaching for himself but for 'the undeliverable, nameless perils' of the great whale.[34]

Enigmatic though Ahab surely is, he just as certainly emerges as a figure of large and tragic proportions. As Ishmael recedes as a figure in the action, Ahab, this 'maimed, maddened, predestinated old man',[35] assumes greater dramatic focus, until there is no release from his annihilative quest for the white whale: 'In his fiery eyes of scorn and triumph, you then saw Ahab in all his fatal pride.' Hounded by his confrontation with the 'personified impersonal', Ahab is driven to defy all that otherness perceived to be over against the self. Writes Brodhead: 'Ahab is obsessively conscious of inhuman supernatural powers. Ordinary reality simply evaporates before his boiling mind as he projects himself out of it to engage in cosmic contests.'[36] Such projection is marvellously rendered in one of *Moby Dick's* most famous chapters, 'The Doubloon', when Ahab, peering into this 'bright coin', says:

> There's something ever egotistical in mountain-tops and towers, and all other grand and lofty things; look here, – three peaks as proud as Lucifer. The firm tower, that is Ahab; the volcano, that is Ahab; the courageous, the undaunted, and victorious fowl, that, too, is Ahab; all are Ahab; and this round gold is but the image of the rounder globe, which, like a magician's glass, to each and every man in turn but mirrors back his own mysterious self.

Yet there is a moment, near the end, when this self-bound vision opens to admit the reality of another self, a tragic, final glimpse when he finds himself able, as Bowen remarks, to forget his anger and answer love with love: 'the Prometheus in him has not wholly yielded to the fiercer Enceladus'.[37] Before he finally crosses the deck, thus ultimately choosing to side with Fedallah, Ahab admits to Starbuck feelings betraying the closest he will ever get to values of the heart. He says, in 'The Symphony': 'Close! stand close to me, Starbuck; let me look into a human eye; it is better than to gaze into sea or sky; better than to gaze upon God. By the green land; by the bright hearthstone! this is the magic glass, man....' But this deeply affecting vision is only momentary; it is Ishmael's identity that survives for, unlike Ahab, he has achieved some sense of equipoise with ambiguity. 'Buoyed up by that coffin', the potentiality for meaning is generated by Ishmael's desire to narrate. Ending the chapter, 'The Castaway', Ishmael writes: 'And in the sequel of the narrative, it will then be seen what like abandonment befell myself.'

VI

Ishmael survives it and resumes his ongoing orphan's life with his questions unanswered. In writing Ahab's book he similarly tests to the utmost the possibility of creating a final fiction, of committing himself to one narrative mode and its determinate vision of reality, but in the end he must return to write a book that includes this as one fiction among many, a book that is more faithful to the uncertainty and variety of 'this strangely mixed affair we call life'.[38]

Ishmael's is a troubled self, 'with the problem of the universe revolving in me'. His quest is to seek a resolution to this cosmological dilemma, but what he discovers time and again during 'this deeply vexed odyssey'[39] is a profound legerdemain of metaphysical proportions. For what Ishmael comes to realise, after contemplation of Moby Dick's whiteness, is a horror that stuns one's imagination: 'Though in many of its aspects this visible world seems formed in love, the invisible spheres were formed in fright.' This is a crucial statement embodying Ishmael's developing sense of reality. What he suspects at this stage is an atheistical void behind appearances. Yet he *does* work through to a conditioned balance as he forgoes any static resolution to his epistemological quest. Implications of this more flexible resolution for Ishmael and the reader will take us to the conclusion of this chapter.

The central problem, certainly, deals with appearance and reality. A sea that appears to be wondrous is realised to be only an ersatz balm covering the depths of reality wherein horror resides. As his mind drifts through images of whiteness, Ishmael finds no example of wonder that does not rest on a transcendent horror. Anything eliciting wonder because of something seemingly good only announces the deeper realisation that it will be ultimately terrible. And this is so whether or not that ultimate manifests itself as absolute and infinite, malicious and hostile, or cold, silent and indifferent. In the following passages from Chapter 42, 'The Whiteness of the Whale', we see Ishmael's awareness that experiences of wonder inform the perceiver of, and finally link with, the deepest of transcendent horrors:

[Y]et for all these accumulated associations, with whatever is sweet, and honorable, and sublime, there yet lurks an elusive

Metaphysical Otherness

something in the innermost idea of this hue, which strikes more of panic to the soul than that redness which affrights in blood.

This elusive quality it is, which causes the thought of whiteness, when divorced from more kindly associations, and coupled with any object terrible in itself, to heighten that terror to the furthest bounds. Witness the white bear of the poles, and the white shark of the tropics; what but their smooth, flaky whiteness makes them the transcendent horrors they are? That ghastly whiteness it is which imparts such an abhorrent mildness, even more loathsome than terrific, to the dumb gloating of their aspect. So that not the fierce-fanged tiger in his heraldic coat can so stagger courage as the white-shrouded bear or shark.

Bethink thee of the albatross whence come those clouds of spiritual wonderment and pale dread, in which that white phantom sails in all imaginations? Not Coleridge first threw that spell; but God's great, unflattering laureate, Nature.

The 'wondrous sight of the ivory *Pequod*' is seen two pages later when 'the thick mists were dimly parted by a huge, vague form'. Any glance at the emerald calm and beauty of the sea now brings with it the perception that sharks with a 'wondrous voracity' lurk beneath the surface.

Quite early in the novel, Ishmael allows: 'Not knowing what is good, I am quick to perceive a horror, and could still be social with it.' Friedman rightly notes that

> at the heart of horror is wonder, and horror and wonder are wedded, as nowhere else, in *Moby-Dick*.... The ultimate terror, to [Ishmael], is the indifference of an absolute that excludes man. Now indefiniteness is not a characteristic of truth but an irrational force that threatens us with annihilation.[40]

Considering the scope and intent of *The Reign of Wonder*, one might be initially surprised to discover that Tanner mentions Melville only briefly. The absence of a chapter on Melville is significant, though not because of Tanner's negligence. Rightly understood, the vision of reality experienced by Ishmael is exactly contrary to the 'myth' of wonder being explored by Tanner. None the less, at one moment he does suggest a central issue of this chapter, and he does so in such a way that it makes Ishmael's vision of reality all the more prescient as a tacit awareness of the twentieth-century reader:

> What all these writers stress in their various ways is the radical importance of a true way of seeing; the generous, open, even naive undulled and reverent eye – as opposed to the self-interested squinting and peering of the greedy utilitarian social eye, and the cold myopia of the scientific, analytical eye. Their ideal is an eye of passive wonder.... But as the wonderer has become more and more alienated, the things miraculously revealed to him are not always such as will leave him 'stupid with wonder': sometimes he is stupified with nausea, sometimes paralysed with horror.[41]

The 'portrait here of innocence and naivety unprepared for the deeper enigmas and shocks of the human condition' is most fully rendered, I believe, when wonder is felt to connote radical insecurity, isolation and the disappearance of God; when wonder no longer heralds a transcendent 'Good' but rather suggests an unmitigated evil lurking beneath the appearance of good. Such expectations of wonder work ironically on the conventional understanding of the reader to thrust him or her back into a world of reality where the 'innocent eye' of the passively wondering child becomes, in William James's famous line, 'the buzzing, booming chaos which is the child's world',[42] which, *at this level of reading*, is Ishmael's world. But if such irony implicates the reader, it may be the reader's experience, too.

To seek out reality one must go to sea, where one may find the whale. However, to come up against this living reality, this Moby Dick, is possibly to find the gaping maw of death. In 'The Chase – First Day', Ahab makes just this discovery:

> But suddenly as he peered down and down into its depths, he profoundly saw a white living spot no bigger than a white weasel, with wonderful celerity uprising, and magnifying as it rose, till it turned, and then there were plainly revealed two long crooked rows of white, glistening teeth, floating up from the undiscoverable bottom. It was Moby Dick's open mouth and scrolled jaw; his vast, shadowed bulk still half blending with the blue of the sea. The glittering mouth yawned beneath the boat like an open-doored marble tomb.

Thus we realise this paradox, or ultimate dilemma: both land and sea become hostile to human existence. Ishmael says in 'Brit':

> For all this appalling ocean surrounds the verdant land, so in the soul of man there lies one insular Tahiti, full of peace ad joy, but encompassed by all the horrors of the half-known life. God keep thee! Push not off from that isle, thou canst never return!

To shelter oneself from 'the tough nature of reality' (as R.W.B. Lewis is wont to put it[43]) is to slight oneself from the full truth. Yet the wondrous world yields a truth perhaps so diabolical that one cannot possibly bear it. Pip, to summon a striking example, goes mad 'when carried down alive to wondrous depths'. Reflecting on Pip's near drowning, Ishmael writes: 'But the awful lonesomeness is intolerable. The intense concentration of self in the middle of such a heartless immensity, my God! who can tell it?' Nearly 100 pages later, he seems to answer his question: 'For whatever is truly wondrous and fearful in man, never yet was put into words or books.' Man will never tell of a truly felt 'heartless immensity' because such a truth is too awesomely inhuman.

For many, this outlook emerges as the tragedy of the modern predicament: numbed by the crisis of modernity, there may be little to assist the self in rebounding from shock after disabusing shock, so few touchstones to inform, to balance the self's sensibility. Mirroring this critical spirit of the 1960s, we find Nathan Scott writing:

> The tragic protagonist is overborne by a sense of shipwreck, a sense of radical fissure or rift in the realm of ultimate reality.... [T]he tragic story is, then, a story of man besieged by hazard and adversity, and of man standing at last amidst shipwreck and defeat: on some forsaken heath or ash-heap the tragic man comes finally to see himself as outmatched and overborne by the terrible, voiceless Mystery of the world. The tragic vision is, in short, an unpalliated vision of shock and crisis, and of man in the extremest possible situation where all guarantees of meaning and security in his pilgrimage on earth have disappeared.[44]

Throughout this pessimistic metaphysic presented by Melville is an Ishmael who somehow maintains some semblance of centrality, no matter how much wondrous horror he feels to the depths of his soul. We hear Ishmael cry out: 'So man's insanity is heaven's sense; and wandering from all mortal reason, man comes at last to that celestial thought, which, to reason, is absurd and frantic; and weal or woe, feels then uncompromised, indifferent as his God.' And yet, Ishmael is never completely overwhelmed by the wonders of the terrible reality he confronts; he never relinquishes 'an intellectual and emotional tie to the ordinary world'.[45] Melville does not submit to nihilism, for *the self survives the voyage to tell of the ambiguities of the quest for certainty*. Never swallowed by a madness such as Ahab's, Ishmael's sensibility cannot rest, for his quest for truth is of a kind that cannot be closed, a 'story that cannot achieve a completion or significance beyond what he himself has discovered in his experience'.[46]

Ishmael's account presses for a sense of observed coexistence with the dual aspects of nature. His confrontations with otherness, he learns, body forth a plural world of both/and rather than either/or. Such experiences can be startling, fearfully strange (recall the tombstones of Father Mapple's chapel, or the apparition of the 'spirit-spout', or 'The Jeroboam's Story'), terribly alienating (think of the cosmic voids betokened by 'the whiteness of the whale'), astonishingly numinous and peacefully secure, or utterly beguiling and mysterious (such as when Ishmael is gripped in moments he calls 'significant darkness'). Because of such experiences, the reader participates in 'Ishmael's insistence on the relativity of perception',[47] and so he hears Ishmael's voice revealing 'a Catskill eagle in some souls that can alike dive down into the blackest gorges, and soar out of them again and become invisible in the sunny spaces' (ch. 96, 'The Try-Works').

The underlying unity of *Moby-Dick* is the responsive sensibility of Ishmael. In the light of this chapter's argument, we may assent to Bert Bender's admission that '*Moby-Dick* is founded in Ishmael's capacity for wonder',[48] but we would have to add that *Moby-Dick* is realised by the reader's participation in the tale told. Ishmael's telling directs the reader to the possibility of a like capacity for wonder. Restless Ishmael has moored his view of the cosmos in an ever-emergent pattern, and it is because of the reader's share in the shuttle of meaning that we are justified in asserting that Ishmael's 'loom is still a-weaving'.[49] Having experienced the otherness of his quest, Ishmael realises his experience in the form of narrative. Ishmael's solitary survival at the end of the tale, Marius Bewley rightly suggests, 'is the validation of his vision'.[50]

Metaphysical Otherness 63

Rather than seeing a confrontation with the whale as the generative source of all meaning, Ishmael's telling secures for the reader the experience of meaning in the strategies of the narrative itself. Once the reader sees the tale as Ishmael's survival after the told quest for final meanings, he or she may better appreciate the degree to which he or she has been ironically implicated throughout the course of the reading. To hold that Ishmael's narrative is retrospective, to distinguish the Ishmael of the action and the later Ishmael of the telling, is to be caught, as a reader, by the levels of the telling.

The recognition of this entanglement offers the reader the experience of his or her own horizon of understanding in the act of interpreting what is beyond (other than) him or herself. The process of reading is part of the meaning; Ishmael offers his narrative to the reader in just this way, though this is not apparent until the reader has completed *Moby-Dick* and has begun it a second time, after the *telos* of the telling has been revealed in the 'Epilogue'. Indeed, at one point in his writing, Ishmael looks up and out at the reader to ask: 'And what are you, reader, but a Loose-Fish and a Fast-Fish, too?' Ishmael's problems are felt meaningfully to be our problems in reading. The reader's realisation that Ishmael is aware of such difficulties for the reader heightens the significance of irony for such self-knowing narration. The telling of *Moby-Dick* is offered by Ishmael as one awesome, grand strategy of self-transcendence, a telling that functions in such a way for us readers as to reveal our participation in 'but a draught of a draught' of a literary universe where one reading can never suffice.

4
Epiphanic Otherness: *Ulysses'* 'Eumaeus' Episode and the Ambush of the Reader's Expectations

Signatures of all things I am here to read.
Stephen Dedalus in *Ulysses*

The journey taken in *Ulysses* is the book itself, and only the reader traverses it entirely.[1]

I

Joyce prefers the human form divine to the divine form human.[2]

In this chapter, situated midway between the metaphysical themes rendered by Melville and the hermeneutic experience elicited from the reader in the work of Iris Murdoch, I wish to discuss a dimension of the pre-eminently modern text, *Ulysses*, a dimension that bears directly on my overall theme of otherness. Though much has been written about the significance of epiphany and the aesthetic intentions of James Joyce, little discussion has been offered to date on the epiphanic mode and its function in the later episodes of *Ulysses*. I have chosen one such episode, 'Eumaeus', in order to give point to the many aspects that come into play for the reader to actualise what for all appearances must be the thematic climax of this richly complex novel. Such 'appearances' are the conventional expectations that have troubled readers for decades, and it is the experience of the displacement of such expectations that I shall call, in this singular instance, epiphanic.

This chapter seeks to discuss, in Joseph Conrad's phrase, a 'moment of awakening', experienced not by a particular character – as one might argue has occurred with Ishmael and as I hope to show does occur with several of Murdoch's narrators – but rather by the reader as he actualises a reading of *Ulysses'* 'Eumaeus' episode. I shall argue that the experience realised by the reader may justly be described as 'epiphanic', traditionally because of Joyce's novel understanding of epiphany, critically because of the significance often attached to the term by sundry literary critics, and thematically as a form of apprehended 'otherness' situated in the body of this essay. As I noted in Chapter 1, the term James Joyce uses for the significant experience of momentary apprehensions of otherness is epiphany. I simply want to look closely at a crucial instance in Joyce's *oeuvre* where the reader is forced to recognise such an apprehension at a time when no character could.

II

> Epiphanies produce an effect that might be called 'the modern sublime'. For while they produce in the reader the emotions named by writers on the sublime... they add an awareness of disparity between the diction and visualization, on the one hand, and the sublime effect on the other. The sense of disparity is particularly acute in Joyce.[3]

For one to move from the 'breathtaking'[4] experience of *Moby-Dick* to a reading of *Ulysses* is to encounter the contrast between a rigorous thematic of the metaphysical voyage spilling over with drama to a thematic of the enviroment of ordinary life, where very little in the nature of plot happens. The idea of epiphany, as rendered in *Ulysses*, in part is the suggestion that the extraordinary arises from and is part of the ordinary universe, and hence there follows for the reader the 'sense of disparity' cited by Langbaum in the above epigraph.

If one were to accept an early view of Robert Scholes (a decade later he finds himself writing of 'structuralist epiphanies'[5]), it would indeed be difficult to speak of an 'epiphanic mode'. According to Scholes's 1964 essay, the notion of epiphany is limited to those instances wherein Joyce set down his 'Epiphanies' – 40 have survived, 53 including duplications – or where Stephen employs the term in a discussion with Cranly in *Stephan Hero*. Because Joyce thereafter shelved the explicit discursive use of the term, critics should do likewise.

My opinion, however, is that the term epiphany – or the experience towards which it points – is perhaps too important to be discarded, for reasons I hope to make clear throughout the following discussion. The situation of indefinite terminological foci is not novel in the ongoing discourse of literary criticism. T. S. Eliot's phrase 'objective correlative' (a later version of the Joycean notion of epiphany) has achieved both popularity and relevance far beyond Eliot's avowed intent or imagination, yet its relevance is not philosophically specific, and it lacks rigour as a concept. Likewise, as we saw above in Chapter 2, Coleridge's discussion of the Primary Imagination and the Secondary Imagination in Chapter 13 of his *Biographia Literaria* yields at best a blurred distinction. Gerard Manley Hopkins's notion of 'inscape' is yet another frequently cited example that comes to mind, and again one finds an indefinite yet not totally vague term. All these concepts survive and prove to be worth consideration, in large measure because of their overriding suggestiveness and felt relevance. They survive as fecund terms relating to the human imagination as she experiences her life-world.

Just so, I find it worthwhile to explore various dimensions of this term 'epiphany', a word first given modern literary currency by Joyce, since it was he who, as M. H. Abrams notes, 'deliberately transfer[ed] the theological term into a naturalistic aesthetic'.[6] Since my interests in this chapter push beyond the way Joyce used the term in *Stephen Hero*, I shall consider applications of this concept which may justify the relevance of it to reader-response criticism.

Now the epiphanies can be taken literally, as events that occurred historically, as concrete facts set down by Joyce in manuscript form before he penned the stories eventually gathered together in *Dubliners*. Many of those transcribed were apparently experienced by Joyce as dream-epiphanies. Scholes suggests that 'their chief significance is in the use Joyce often made of them in his later works'.[7] That is to say, in and of themselves the 40 'Epiphanies' do not amount to much as isolated and disembodied forms of palpable meaning, of vortices of meaning. They become charged with significance only when lodged within the narrative structures of Joyce's fiction. Thus Joyce initially inserted them, Ellmann informs us, 'in *Stephen Hero* to aid in the exposures and illuminations of that novel'.[8]

One may turn to the only work of Joyce where a formal definition of epiphany is touched upon: *Stephen Hero*. Stephen explains to the passive listener Cranly that by 'epiphany' he means 'a sudden spiritual manifestation'. This is the third of three stages of aesthetic apprehension. First, one descries the physical presence of an object as one thing, as an image having wholeness of *integritas*; secondly, one apprehends the aesthetic image in view of its symmetry and rhythm of structure – in a word, its *consonantia*. *Claritas* is the third principle of perception, and it suggests the 'radiance' or 'whatness' or *'quidditas'*[9] of the object. The most explicit formulation of epiphany in Joyce's writings is the following passage:

> *Claritas* is *quidditas*. After the analysis which discovers the second quality the mind makes the only logically possible synthesis and discovers the third quality. This is the moment which I call epiphany. First we recognise that the object is *one* integral thing, then we recognise that it is an organized composite structure, a *thing* in fact: finally, when the relation of the parts is exquisite, when *the parts are adjusted* to the special point, we recognise that it is *that* thing which it is. Its soul, its whatness, leaps to us from the vestment of its appearance. The soul of the commonest object, the structure of which is so adjusted, seems to us radiant. The object achieves its epiphany.[10]

We note the especial emphasis placed on the object as object-perceived, object-epiphanised, object as showing forth or illumining some sense of meaning and signification initially hidden, not seen. That is, epiphany is here conceived 'solely as a quality of experience'. Thus, the relationship between the objective and subjective aspects of the epiphany are not clarified. The point, nevertheless, is that somehow a natural object exceeds its 'naturalistic capacity'. Such 'a sudden spiritual manifestation', Stephen elaborates, may be found 'in the vulgarity of speech or of gesture or in a memorable phase of the mind itself'. A manifestation of this quality, suggests Morris Beja, is 'out of proportion to the significance or strictly logical relevance of whatever produces it'.[11]

In works written after *Stephen Hero*, the objective and subjective aspects are given more point, as the epiphanies progress toward more symbolic dimensions of character and atmosphere. It is important to understand that the notion of epiphany evolves in complexity and sophistication because of language, a point worth recalling when we undertake a critical inquiry of the nature of the 'Eumaeus' episode below. The reader becomes sensitive to the artistically wrought form rendering the epiphanic. By the time one experiences a reading of *Ulysses* and *Finnegans Wake*, one no longer finds an epiphanic dimension residing merely in the non-literary 'sudden spiritual manifestations' of a character's fictive life. Indeed, one finds in *Ulysses*, says S.L. Goldberg, that it broadens to the suggestion of a 'gesture', 'an act of the total personality of the maker, which "renders visible" what is there to be revealed in reality – an entelechy" – by and in the medium of a constructed "structural rhythm" '.[12]

It is the vocation of the artist, Stephen declares, to render the manifestations, the revelations of the nature of reality, as forms of 'intelligible matter' by way of 'sensible matter'. The epiphanies involve a conjunction of subject and object, and thereby show forth meaningfully, in the consequent synthesis, as *claritas*, in a larger whole.

What we have, then, is an epiphanic moment of sudden coherence, an experience embodied in a work of art, a secular moment charged with immanent meaning, giving one – be he or she the author (Joyce certainly 'felt' various epiphanies and wrote them down), character (Stephen, throughout *A Portrait of the Artist as a Young Man*; Gabriel Conroy, at the end of 'The Dead'; Stephen, Molly and especially Leopold Bloom in *Ulysses*), or reader – for a brief time, accession to that which is felt to be a dislodging of the veil of appearance of an object and a revelation of its 'whatness', its purchase of *quidditas*. The experience may be mundane in a vulgar way, or it may be joyful, indeed cosmic, whereby the sudden disclosure suffuses the mundane with transfiguring significance.

III

> From the propositional and 'metaphysical' point of view, the nature of reality is intrinsically hidden. Within the limits of our finite perceiving it must be 'grasped' in the perspectival and contextual modes – that is to say mythically, metaphorically, symbolically.... There is always 'Something More' beyond the formal inclusions of our closely threaded premises.[13]

The above suggestion of Stephen's theory of art, artist and aesthetics is meant to be a critical preface to the following discussion of the 'Eumaeus' episode, a reading offered in the light of the notion of epiphany. We have seen that Joyce's term epiphany denotes several emphases: Joyce's concept of the function of the artist, his theories of aesthetics, and most importantly for the present argument, his understanding of epiphany when placed in the context of his novels. When situated in this context, the concept of epiphany points to a phenomenon available in all human experience, and not just in the province of the artist.

Dramatically, Joyce portrays characters' minds engaged in the apprehension of epiphanies – moments of meaning apprehended as they burst forth from the ordinary in life, or phrases in a book that draw together clusters of meaning. Anthony Burgess once noted that Joyce 'saw his function as priestlike – the solemnisation of drab days and the sanctification of the ordinary'.[14]

What Joyce's idea of epiphany amounts to is a theory of perception, a confidence that the individual mind can rise above solipsism and actually apprehend the objects of the world, as Stephen discovers and thinks, 'there without end, world without end'. This is another way of saying that one is able to experience the world as *other* or, as Stephen would say of the physical world, as 'ineluctable'. The notion of the epiphanic suggests a manifestation of reality breaking into human experience, usually suddenly, always truthfully. Drawn into an articulated aesthetic, we can hear echoes as various as Heidegger and Murdoch. For example, a contemporary Heideggerian critic and originating influence for the field of religion and literature, Hopper, writes: 'It is through the art work that we are enabled to see what a thing is as it is in itself.'[15] And Murdoch offers the following characteristic statement in *The Sovereignty of Good*: 'The greatest art...shows us the world...with a clarity which startles and delights us simply because we are not used to looking at the real world at all.'[16]

As noted in Chapter 2, it has been traditionally helpful to view the reality of a novel as three-fold. There is the fictive world of the characters, in which they discover and experience that which is consitutive of their reality. There is the fabulating 'gesture' of the artist as he creates, whereby he expresses through language *his* apprehension of reality. And also, there is the very real, if mysterious, engagement experienced by the audience as it is enjoined to take an imaginative leap from its commonplace reality into the veritable phenomenon of the 'otherness' of the work of literature. Goldberg is correct to bring out the following distinction:

> epiphanies... are at one level acts of apprehension made by the characters,... acts of understanding in everyday life. But they are also, at a higher power, as it were, the artist's apprehensions of the significance of those acts (their forms or 'quiddities' perhaps). The characters perceive meanings in life; we are shown further meanings in their perceptions.[17]

I would insist that we, too, as readers, may encounter the quality of epiphany rendered by the event of the artist's creation. Therefore, as have Gabriel Conroy and Stephen and Leopold Bloom, and as has Joyce himself, so may we too be present to the perception of the manifestation of radical immanence, a possibility that, when rendered in literary works of art, has interested religion and literature critics such as Stanley Romaine Hopper and Nathan Scott. And, accordingly, we find Giles Gunn putting the matter of the lyrical epiphany in the following striking way: 'The discovery itself is of the astonishing numinousness of things as they are, of the rich liminality of ... "the ordinary universe".'[18]

Suffice it to say that there are several presentations of epiphanies recognised by nearly all critics conversant with Joyce's methods, aims and techniques; most occur early in Joyce's work, but several survive through *Ulysses*. A realisation of the significance of the epiphany and its role clarifies many of Joyce's stylistic manoeuvrings, and these should be kept in mind as we ready ourselves for the 'Eumaeus' episode, to be discussed on its own terms presently.

The reader finds Joyce focusing on apparently trivial incidents. Several critics point out that he relies structurally on key scenes of revelation (for example, at the end of a chapter, as in *A Portrait*, or at the end of a group of three chapters, as in *Ulysses*). This affects the way these or other scenes or events bring together a number of his most important themes. Indeed, not a few critics maintain that Joyce's main themes are carried forward chiefly through climatic epiphanies. Joyce's emphasis on the recollection of previous scenes or events or his foreshadowings of the future are informed by the epiphany. Recall Stephen's vision of the wading girl near the end of the penultimate chapter of *A Portrait of the Artist as a Young Man*, a memorable experience which yields a feeling of promise and freedom for the young artist alienated from both his nation and his church. Bring to mind the scene in the Nighttown episode of *Ulysses*, where Stephen remembers the pandying he received from a priest in school 16 years before; or, in the same episode, his vision of his dead mother.

Joyce's epiphanies, these 'moments of heightened awareness, secular illuminations',[19] are seen by David Hayman as an 'essentially realistic tool'. I would suggest that the epiphanic mode *functions* to involve the reader as accomplice, as co-creator (an image I shall return to later). What I wish to stress at this moment is the inherent *referentiality* of the epiphanic mode. Thus, we are not surprised that Jon Lanham locates and speaks of an 'epiphanous agency' in Joyce's fiction. In a frequently cited article, Lanham writes that 'an epiphany is to be judged by its effect on the reader, not the character, and thus is dependent on its rhetorical frame'.[20] The 'Eumaeus' episode, I shall argue below, is epiphanic to the degree that it involves the reader as co-creator, leading him or her to an 'earned apprehension of radiance through active contemplation'. For what the *reader discovers* through the experience of reading 'Eumaeus' is a recovery of the significance of the individual act of apprehension. Although such significance is prominent in the first half of *Ulysses* among the characters themselves, it is displaced by the narrative devices Joyce chose to use in the last nine episodes, techniques which yield more arbitrary points of view.

IV

Every tale implies a teller. But not every tale implies an *author*.[21]

Before we concentrate on a close reading of the 'Eumaeus' episode and, later on, 'the tale of the telling', we must acknowledge a return to the significance of the teller and the telling of the tale first discussed in Chapter 3. The accounts of *Moby-Dick*, *A Severed Head* and *The Black Prince* are offered by first-person narrators; only one of the 18 episodes comprising *Ulysses* – that of 'Cyclops' – is so rendered. Again, there is difference in this seeming similarity. We sense that characterisation in *Moby-Dick* is always functioning in the shadow of metaphysical themes. For Murdoch, characters instead resist reduction to the service of types or illustrations and hold greater kinship to the realist tradition of nineteenth-century British fiction. It is not surprising that Joyce, in *Ulysses*, has it both ways. Stephen Dedalus and Leopold Bloom in the first half of the book are felt to be firmly grounded in 'the rock of Ithaca', roundly and realistically presented. But they diminish in view as the arranger forces the reader and language itself as deceptive to enter the central action of the narrative. As David Hayman remarks, 'plot and engrossing action become almost vestigial'.[22] The obvious result is that the reader's role is increased the further he proceeds in *Ulysses* because 'Joyce has changed the focus of his interest from his characters to his styles',[23] a point thoroughly brought home by Michael Groden's work in *'Ulysses' in Progress*. By the time the reader confronts the 'Eumaeus' episode, he is fully familiar with Joyce's 'massive unwillingness to get on with it and tell a simple linear tale',[24] as Robert Scholes has noted in *Structuralism in Literature*. None the less, Stephen and Bloom may continue to figure significantly for the reader. 'Joyce's characters', writes Iser, 'begin to take on a life of their own the moment we, the readers, begin to react to them, and our reactions consist of an attempt to grasp and hold fast to their individuality.'[25]

The reality of character figures significantly in my understanding of the 'Eumaeus' episode. We could do no better than to take Bloom as a relevant illustration of this relationship between characterisation and reader. Rather than proposing, as many critics have done, that Bloom is an unexceptional, a common man, it is surely more accurate to note that Bloom is uncommon precisely because of his ability to care for others. Unlike Stephen, he is not questing for existence. Rather, Bloom has existence, and thus he has the moral equipoise to allow people to be 'other', without sentimentalisation. The reader knows this before beginning the 'Eumaeus' episode, and it is against this charitable characterisation of Bloom acknowledged throughout the previous episodes of the text that the reader measures the narrator's deceitful tone. This tone or attitude of the narrator is felt in his endless descriptions, forms of expression which the reader recognises as a sundering of, a violation of, the novel's established decorum. Thus, the function of style in 'Eumaeus': the reader must acknowledge that the style of 'Eumaeus' – as with the styles found in *all* the later episodes – works against the previous realistic context elaborated in the first nine episodes of *Ulysses*. With this acknowledgment comes the recognition that style and technique assume a greater role in the function of meaning because of their impact on the reader. I shall return to this topic in section VI.

Two areas of significance emerge for the reader in the 'Eumaeus' episode. The first is the dramatic fact that 'Eumaeus' occurs after 'Circe', and *the reader finds him or herself confronting that liminal world* 'where dream departs into reality', as Gerald Bruns has aptly phrased it.[26] (One might broaden this idea by stating that 'Eumaeus' occurs immediately before 'Ithaca', and thus note *the 'Eumaeus' episode as a region of liminality residing between* the two ostensible climaxes of *Ulysses*: in 'Circe', Bloom ends his search for his son; in 'Ithaca', the story climaxes when Bloom takes Stephen home, Stephen chooses to leave, Bloom faces his problem with Molly.) The second is that the readers' desire for a purposeful relationship between Stephen and Bloom becomes thematic, and the reader's expectation of a resolution to the plot of *Ulysses* is ambushed. It is displaced by the epiphanic revelation of language itself, in all its forceful guile, showing itself as itself, and thereby holding out to the reader the experience, as Maurice Natanson would have it, of 'language epiphaniz[ing] transcendent meanings through its own instrumentality'.[27]

The reader is required to displace the power of the language offered by the guiding intelligence of the narrator, that 'selecting, arranging, and self-proclaiming figure'.[28] The reader struggles against the narrator's rhetoric because it undermines our relationship, our concern and interest for Bloom and Stephen. This is why it is incorrect to propose, as many have insisted, that the episode is rendered from Bloom's own viewpoint – in his language, perhaps, but as a representation of Bloom's sensibility, hardly, for it lacks his honesty. As I noted earlier, we recoil against the dehumanising technique of 'Eumaeus', and find ourselves all the more fervently asserting the human dignity being stifled by the narrative process that orchestrates the episode's theme of linguistic duplicity. 'Because one wants to feel with the characters', French remarks, 'one goes on pumping in blood.'[29] The reader, to echo Iser here, has to fill in the gap with feeling. Indeed, this act provokes an interesting question; the reader might wonder: to what degree has the narrator been effaced? Just what aesthetic blank has the reader filled to have realised the potential meaning just experienced, the coming together of Bloom and Stephen?

V

> The sense of a text is always more than itself.
>
> Tzvetan Todorov[30]

The style of the sixteenth chapter of *Ulysses* reveals the condition, and something of the nature, of Bloom and Stephen. Joyce called it 'relaxed', but one might more properly find it clumsy, duplicitous, stale and as full of fatigue as those events and characters it tiresomely describes. The style is self-conscious, obscurant, and yet surprisingly comic. It holds us in part because of the extraordinary skill mustered by Joyce to bring it off. Hugh Kenner points out in *Joyce's Voices*:

> There is no one... who could write three consecutive sentences of it, fatigued or alert. It is open to wonder whether any episode cost Joyce such pains, plumbing depths of expressive infelicity most of us have not the talent even to conceive.[31]

In this episode wit pales, understanding recedes, all is prolix and weary. Except for the tall tales energetically proffered by the windy sailor, little happens. Rather than encountering, say, the 'frisky agitation'[32] brought off by the arranger in 'Wandering Rocks', we have the wearisome fables unfolded in the cabman's shelter by the sailor, cozening both his listeners and the reader. The climax of *Ulysses* already met in the 'Circle' episode, the following chapter must, in some wise, be anti-climactic. The Odyssey over, the walk home now begins.

And yet... And yet, suggested within this early-morning 'constabular style' is an event of ultimate import. Thematically, the entire novel has been pointing toward the meeting of fatherly Bloom and fatherless Stephen. Throughout this sixteenth day in June 1904 they have crossed paths. Stephen is passed by Bloom as the latter heads, in a procession, to Paddy Dignam's funeral; they almost meet at the newspaper office, but Bloom steps out just before Stephen enters; they nearly meet again at the library; they barely miss each other at the bookstall (where Bloom has just purchased *Sweets of Sin* for Molly); and finally they encounter each other at the hospital. Concerned for the welfare of drunken Stephen, Bloom impulsively follows him to Bella Cohen's brothel, even though he wonders why he does so. The swirling phantasmagoric events of nighttown in the 'Circe' episode culminate in an apparition: Bloom, standing over the knocked-down Stephen, has a vision of his dead son Rudy:

> (Silent, thoughtful, alert, [Bloom] stands on guard, his fingers at his lips in the attitude of secret master. Against the dark wall a figure appears slowly, a fairy boy of eleven, a changeling, kidnapped, dressed in an Eton suit with glass shoes and a little bronze helmet, holding a book in his hand. He reads from right to left inaudibly, smiling, kissing the page.)
> BLOOM
> (wonderstruck, calls inaudibly) Rudy!
> RUDY
> (gazes, unseeing, into Bloom's eyes and goes on reading, kissing, smiling. He has a delicate mauve face. On his suit he has diamond and ruby buttons. In his free left hand he holds a slim ivory cane with a violet bowknot. A white lambkin peeps out of his waistcoat pocket.)

This moving presentation concretely depicts Bloom's deep psychological need for a son, his powerful sense of loss for Rudy (who died nearly eleven years before), and signifies for Bloom and the reader the association between Rudy and Stephen. It is, surely, a genuine epiphany for Bloom. It is with this association freshly rendered that *Ulysses* moves immediately into the last triptych, *Nostos*.

Ever emotionally reticent, Joyce does not allow a full-blown fusion when Bloom hands Stephen his hat and ashplant – nothing, at least, in the order of a classical scene of recognition, or anagnorisis. Indeed, this fortuitous coming-together seems, in 'Eumaeus', to be anything but a meeting. The *content* of their attempts at conversation holds little of interest for the reader/listener. When attention is being given, the focus of the subject – be it religion, politics, music or food – is blurred, and real communication misfires. The two, finally meeting, have immense trouble reducing differences, being 'poles apart', a fact that Richard Kain calls 'the cruel distance between them'.[33] The incompetent prose style, again, is pertinent to this reality of imperfect intimacy.[34]

Banal and bumbling though Bloom may be, the consciousness of Bloom rendered in this episode still shows his immense ability to *care* for another human being. However instinctual and inchaote is Bloom's sense of fatherly concern for Stephen, the reader knows that their meeting is significant. Bloom is revealed – fatigue notwithstanding – to be eager to make contact. We find him, friendly and unoffending, bearing the presence of unassuming decency. Consciousness expanded, he can devote full attention to the welfare of homeless, hungry Stephen.

The Homeric parallel is this: the Phaecian sailors have put the sleeping Odysseus on the shores of Ithaca. Upon awakening, he is bewildered as to his whereabouts, until Athena appears to provide bearings and council. Thus prepared, Odysseus attires himself with beggar's garments for disguise and goes to meet Eumaeus, his faithful swineherd. Gracious and hospitable, despite Odysseus's 'cock-and-bull' tale of his identity and his journey to Ithaca, Eumeaus receives his guest until the arrival of Telemachus. Revealing himself to his son, they depart, reunited, with a planned approach to their home, a house presently beleaguered and endangered by Penelope's suitors.

Bloom, at the beginning of the 'Eumaeus' episode, is initially a bit remonstrant with Stephen '*re* the dangers of nighttown, women of ill fame and swell mobsmen'.[35] Stephen, for the most part, remains silent before this 'fussy solicitude'.

After giving an old acquaintance, Corley, some money, Stephen echoes a central theme of the episode: 'I have no place to sleep myself' (*U*, 504). And Bloom promptly responds, after Corley fades into the darkness:

> But, talking about things in general, where, added he with a smile, will you sleep yourself? Walking to Sandycove is out of the question. And even supposing you did you won't get in after what occurred at Westland Row station. Simply fag out there for nothing. I don't mean to presume to dictate to you in the slightest degree but why did you leave your father's house? (*U*, 507)

Stephen's answer, 'To seek my misfortune', passes beyond Bloom's understanding, but concern for Stephen's welfare is still foremost in Bloom's mind, so he suggests that perhaps Stephen could still go back home. 'There was no response forthcoming to the suggestion, however', Joyce tells us, 'Stephen's mind's eye being too busily engaged in repicturing his family hearth the last time he saw it' (*U*, 620). This registering of a painful memory of his family's poor, desperate state emphasies Stephen's felt homelessness and his alienation from his irresponsible father.

Bloom, ever friendly and full of interest, lets drop two more suggestions about his suspicions of Mulligan and reflects again about Stephen as an intellectual who has yet to realise his potential:

> Except it simply amounts to one thing and he is what they call picking your brains, he ventured to throw out.
> The guarded glance of half solicitude, half curiosity augmented by friendliness which he gave at Stephen's at present morose expression of features did not throw a flood of light, none at all in fact on the problem as to whether he had let himself be badly bamboozled to judge by two or three low-spirited remarks he let drop or the other way about, saw through the affair and for some reason or other best known to himself allowed matters to more or less. Grinding poverty did have that effect and he more than conjectured that, high educational abilities though he possessed, he experienced no little difficulty in making both ends meet. (*U*, 507–8)

Bloom is, of course, preparing the way in his mind for later ruminations about helping Stephen realise his artistic gifts.

Entering the cabman's shelter, they find themselves in an Odyssean world of mistaken identities, pretenders, lies and mysterious names. Two principle characters (the principal talkers) emerge: 'Skin-the-Goat, Fitzharris, the invincible' and a red-bearded sailor, W.B. Murphy. Both have false identities, and Bloom ultimately suspects as much. The keeper, although eager to stir up notions of Irish revolution, is not the driver of the cab in which the Invincibles escaped after committing the infamous Phoenix Park murders in 1882. He suggests that the political leader, Parnell, is not dead and will return, but Bloom will have none of it; even if Parnell were alive, Bloom decides it would be best for him not to return anyway.

Throughout the scene in the shelter, Bloom encourages Stephen to drink some (undrinkable) coffee and have a bit of bun. Even such a simple gesture as this is described lengthily: 'For which reason he encouraged Stephen to proceed with his eyes while he did the honours by surreptitiously pushing the cup of what was temporarily supposed to be called coffee gradually nearer him' (*U*, 509).

Stephen, still 'suffering from dead lassitude generally', points out that 'Sounds are impostures.... Shakespeares were as common as Murphies. What's in a name?' (*U*, 509). The most obvious imposter in the episode, named Murphy (thus, a name so common as to be 'no-man') strikes up a banter filled with far-fetched fables. These set Bloom's mind on a mini-odyssesy of its own, wandering from the locale of the South American Indian hut (pictured on Murphy's postcard) to such hopes as the Tweedy-Flower Opera Company. He asks this Ulysses Pseudangelos (Joyce's term for this false Ulysses) if he had sailed near Molly's birthplace, Europa point, but he gets a short denial: ' "I'm tired of all them rocks in the sea, he said, and boats and ships. Salt junk all the time." Tired, seemingly, he ceased' (*U*, 515).

None the less, sincere though Bloom's intentions are, communication is still failing with Stephen. Talk of the 'necessary evil' of prostitution leads them to a discussion of the soul's existence. Stephen's response is obscure to the less-schooled mind of Bloom:

> They tell me on the best authority [the soul] is a simple substance and therefore incorruptible. It would be immortal, I understand, but for the possibility of its annihilation by its First Cause Who, from all I can hear, is quite capable of adding that to the number of His other practical jokes, *corruptio per se* and *corruptio per accidens* both being exluded by court etiquette.   (*U*, 518)

Bloom's response is ludicrous, for he is 'no hand at following Daedalian flights of fancy': 'Mr Bloom thoroughly acquiesced in the general gist of this though the mystical finesse involved was a bit out of his sublunary depth still he felt bound to enter a demurrer on the head of simple' (*U*, 518).

From this Bloom plunges into a pseudo-scientific notion that maunders from questioning how frequently one finds a 'simple' soul to the implausibility of a supernatural God – all of which, as Bloom presents the argument, makes little reasonable sense. What follows is a statement of the central conflict of the episode: 'On this knotty point however the views of the pair, poles apart as they were both in schooling and everything else with the marked difference in their respective ages, clashed' (*U*, 518). As the evening drags on, 'Interest, however, was starting to flag somewhat all round' (*U*, 521).

Bloom relates the afternoon's incident with the Citizen in Barney Kiernan's pub, altering the facts to his own credit, saying that he appeased the wrath of the Citizen with his wise words about Jewry. Stephen, seeing Bloom's entreating gaze, recognises him for the first time: '*Ex quibus*, Stephen mumbled in a noncommittal accent, their two or four eyes conversing, *Christus* or Bloom his name is or after all any other, *secundum carnem*' (*U*, 525). Stephen's statement associates Bloom both to Christ ('And from that race [the Israelites] is Christ'), and to all humanity ('or, after all, any other, according to the flesh'). And Bloom, accordingly, sounds, for the moment, very much the humanitarian: 'But with a little goodwill all around. It's all very find to boast of mutual superiority but what about mutual equality? I resent violence and intolerance in any shape or form' (*U*, 525).

But communication again refuses to hold, and Bloom lapses into an absurdly wordy, confusing and finally senseless exposition about history, Jews, Spain, Cromwell, the Turks, America and a smattering of his economic theory of 'all creeds and classes *pro rata* having a comfortable tidysized income' (*U*, 526). Stephen's inner response is quite characteristic: 'Over his untastable apology for a cup of coffee, listening to this synopsis of things in general, Stephen stared at nothing in particular. He could hear, of course, all kinds of words changing colour like those crabs about Ringsend in the morning' (*U*, 526). This reaction echoes Stephen's earlier comment, 'Sounds are impostures', and indicates the atmosphere in which verbosity may ambush genuine concern. Presently his egocentricity undiminished, Stephen befuddles Bloom with this forthright assertion: 'But I suspect.... that Ireland must be important because it belongs to me' (*U*, 527), and adds curtly. 'We can't change the country. Let us change the subject' (*U*, 527).

Throughout such confusion, Bloom's consciousness refuses to be blunted. He feels deeply Stephen's rebuke, but does not resent him for it. Instead, Bloom reflects on the possiblities of Stephen's difficult life as an artist:

Probably the home life to which Mr B attached the utmost importance had not been all that was needful or he hadn't been familiarised with the right sort of people. With a touch of fear for the young man beside him whom he furtively scrutinized wih an air of some consternation remembering he had just come back from Paris, the eyes more especially reminding him forcibly of father and sister, failing to throw much light on the subject, however, he brought to mind instances of cultured fellows that promised so brilliantly nipped in the bud of premature decay and nobody to blame but themselves. However, reverting to the original, there were on the other hand others who had forced their way to the top from the lowest rung by the aid of their bootstraps. Sheer force of natural genuis, that. With brains, sir. (*U*, 527–8).

Such ruminations stir in Bloom dreams of cultivating a friendship with Stephen. His affection grows, and after showing a picture of Molly, he becomes more optimistic: 'The vicinity of the young man he certainly relished, educated, *distingué* and impulsive into the bargain, far and away the pick of the bunch, though you wouldn't think he had it in him yet you would. Besides he said the picture was handsome which, say what you like, it was' (*U*, 534). Completely attending to Stephen, Bloom reflects:

> To think of him house and homeless, rooked by some landlady worse than any stepmother, was really too bad at his age. The queer suddenly things he popped out with attracted the elder man who was several years the other's senior or like his father. (*U*, 536).

Now aware of Stephen's immediate need for food, Bloom feels not the separateness, but a sense of fusion, of a coming together: 'Though they didn't see eye to eye in everything a certain analogy there somehow was as if both their minds were travelling, so to speak, in the one train of thought' (*U*, 536). Bloom's ensuing thoughts show how much this friendship promises to mean for him: 'All kinds of Utopian plans were flashing through his (Bloom's) busy brain' (*U*, 538). A 'tentative singleness' begins to take hold.

Perhaps, instead of being obtusely intellectual, Stephen finally attempts to speak to Bloom's bourgeois mind, rather than over it: 'One thing I never understood, he said to be original on the spur of the moment. Why they put tables upside down at night, I mean chairs upside down, on the tables in cafes' (*U*, 539).

Ready now to leave the cabman's shelter for his 'diggings', Bloom suggests: 'It will (the air) do you good, Bloom said, meaning also the walk, in a moment. The only thing is to walk then you'll feel a different man. Come. It's not far. Lean on me' (*U*, 539). In so doing, Stephen is now aware of physical contact: 'Yes, Stephen said uncertainly because he thought he felt a strange kind of flesh of a different man approach him, sinewless and wobbly and all that' (*U*, 539).

Music, as a topic, arises, along with the expected assortment of misquoted information and diverging tastes. Yet, nearing the end of 'Eumaeus', such problems of communication no longer seem to be pushing the two apart. Stephen, at least tentatively, accepts the fellowship of Bloom as, we know, Bloom wholeheartedly accepts the wayward Stephen. They walk towards Eccles Street 'Bloom fatherly, Stephen what he is'.[36]

The last paragraph of the episode further suggests this possible communion of souls between Bloom and Stephen. These 'two noctambules', now together, intimate in support, are last viewed fully engaged in discussion as they walk to Bloom's house *'to be married'*:

> The driver never said a word, good, bad or indifferent, but merely watched the two figures, *as he sat on his low-backed car*, both black, one full, one lean, walk towards the railway bridge, *to be married by Father Maher*. As they walked they at times stopped and walked again continuing their tete-a-tete (which of course he was utterly out of) about sirens, enemies of man's reason, mingled with a number of other topics of the same category, usurpers, historical cases of the kind while the man in the sweeper car or you might as well call it the sleeper car who in any case couldn't possibly hear because they were too far simply sat in his seat near the end of lower Gardiner Street *and looked after their lowbacked car*. (*U*, 543)

Perhaps we behold a limen of the epiphanic in our experience of this passage.

Surely, the large point to be made is that the reader's encounter with the turgid style of the 'Eumaeus' episode proceeds in anything but an epiphanic manner. Of course, the reader may consider the episode in its entirety as an example of what Ellmann describes as an 'unpalatable' epiphany, an extended example 'of fatuity or imperceptiveness'.[37] Bloom's conversations are certainly 'fatuous'. But it is all the more remarkable that Joyce chose such a style in which to couch the revelation, the *quidditas*, of all that toward which *Ulysses* has been pointing.

What we readers are left with in the closing presentation of 'Eumaeus' is a fillip of the numinous. Joyce has prepared us for this epiphany throughout the episode – indeed, throughout the whole of *Ulysses*. He has done this by the progressive development of the novel's central theme, by indirection with his stylistic devices, and finally, unwittingly, by the driver 'as he sat on his low-backed car'. It is, I would suggest, our epiphany, our 'happening', a disclosure of something meaningful, of liminal dimensions, about our reality as we engage in it by way of our quickened imagination during the act of reading. Joyce has succeeded, for we are participating in 'something more' than the ordinary, bodied forth by way of the ordinary.

VI

> As language approached, reality seemed rather to withdraw than to come closer.[38]

> From the reader's side, the question is one of expectations.[39]

I call for nothing more from the term 'epiphany' than that it suggest, with Ellmann, 'sudden, unlooked-for turns of experience'.[40] I have suggested in Chapter 3 that otherness may be characterised as all that is perceived to lie outside the self, beyond the self: the non-self, if you will. One can also suggest that a book itself might be viewed as a form of otherness to the degree that it resists, or remains independent of, the reader's participation in the matter of meaning. It is precisely this narrative entanglement with the duplicitous veil of impersonality and voiced falsehood in 'Eumaeus' that brings into play the epiphanic horizon of the reader in his voyage 'into the incertitude of the void'. The epiphanic mode gains in significance when we recognise that, just as the post-structural suasion of critical theory urges a model of the reader as active rather than passive, so too this mode is not passive, but rather acknowledges that 'an epiphany is an earned apprehension'.

Bloom and Stephen, awesomely muted though their meeting may be, have come together, though this act achieves significance because of the reader's engagement and despite the sundering intentions of the language. We feel at the end of 'Eumaeus', as we watch Bloom and Stephen walk away from out interests and out of the world into the cold of interstellar space, that their unwitting portraits of life lived have shown us a fuller measure of the world's potential in partial glimpses, 'pieces of the truth', the sum of which the reader has participated in and a truth no character in *Ulysses* has realised at any one time. Another way to say this is to suggest that the convergence of Bloom ('the conscious reactor against the void of incertitude'; *U*, 694) and Stephen (who intends to 'hold to the now, the here, through which all future plunges to the past'; *U*, 238) is symbolic, but they themselves remain unaware of its significance; the meaning happens to the reader.

The recognition of the 'happening' offers the reader the experience of his own horizon of understanding in the act of interpreting what is beyond (other than) himself. A recent statement of Jonathan Culler, in *The Pursuit of Signs*, is relevant to this observation: 'The meaning of a work is its answers to the questions posed by a horizon of expectations.'[41] What is 'revealed' is the recognition by the reader of his own participation in the meaning of the text: 'The reader's epiphany is set within a slightly larger framework [than that of the character] which includes the character's epiphany as well as its context', writes James Maddox.[42] The moment when the reader recognises himself as accomplice in the action of the episode, as a figure realising the theme of the text offered by the narrator – it is this moment of self-discovery offered by the act of reading the 'Eumaeus' episode that may be described as epiphanic. We find ourselves mirroring the paradigmatic event present throughout Joyce's *oeuvre* when we are engaged as co-creators of this episode, not as passive readers but by our active mode of apprehension.

Of all the extant criticism I have been able to examine, one paragraph brings together the most relevant description of those elements playing a crucial role in this chapter's argument. Charles Rossman writes in a recent essay:

> Joyce has arranged the facts in [*Ulysses*] so that the reader is led toward complex, epiphanic, narrative moments which reveal a situation, a circumstance, or a character but leave their 'meaning...still un-uttered'. The reader must engage [this] book by attending closely to the literary facts, 'these present things', in order to go beyond them to their meanings. In particular, the reader's task is to discover the potential meanings of the epiphanic moments.[43]

To do this, the reader must engage the self-reflexivity of the 'tale of the telling', must recognise what Brook Thomas describes as 'the second plane of action between ourselves and the arranger'.[44] Through the act of re-reading, the reader repeats with a difference the flushing out of the 'tale of the telling' from the naturalistic plane of action, the play of language itself when unhinged from the descriptive level traditionally binding the reader's conventional expectations. Thomas expresses the difference of the two levels thus:

> Read as if spoken by the dummy narrator the chapter's words still work on the naturalistic level; they continue to advance the 'story'. But while pretending to give us a quotidian naturalistic plot the words of each chapter unmask themselves. In other words, the words of *Ulysses* sustain two 'tales'. Read as if generated by the dummy narrator of each chapter the words tell the naturalistic plot; read as if generated by the protean narrator of the entire book the very same words tell a self-reflexive tale of the telling which exposes the masquerade of the naturalistic plot's narrator, story, and language.[45]

The structured perspective through which the reader is engaged to adopt the arranger's standpoint in order to fulfill the author's intentions is unlike the style of any other episode in *Ulysses*. We have seen that both the placement of 'Eumaeus' in the overall schema and the theme of the episode present peculiar difficulties for the reader who has been through more than 600 pages of changing narrative styles, where he has seen 'Bloom and Stephen, born of other narrators in previous episodes'.[46]

Thus, one of the baffling features of 'Eumaeus' for the reader is the difficulty of understanding the nature (the mask adopted, the mood through which expression is rendered) of the narrator implied by the style, the technique of the narrative, by the acts of interpretation performed in his telling of this episode. Certainly the ironic elements of 'Eumaeus' force the act of interpretative resolution on to the reader, an act that the arranger makes every effort to hinder. But not any solution will do for, as careful readers preceding us have noted, crucial hints for keeping proper interpretative perspective have been strategically imbedded in the text of the arranger's tale.

The degree of reader provocation is at first reading out of all proportion to the exhausted stasis thematically rendered in this episode. The effect of this stylistic mode of presentation is to push into the fading distance the two characters with whom we have travelled for so long, and also to interrupt or ambush the reader's attention to the novel's narrative events, to interrupt what James

Maddox calls 'the underground current – the reader's own interest'.[47]

We are struck immediately by the fact that, even from the first line of 'Eumaeus', we are not returning to the fundamental, basic style of the first six episodes. Our suspicions are well founded, for the narrator's style is invariable, and the authorial insistence that his language cover over the events of the plot is unrelenting. The teller provides a sustained imbalance for the reader. Iser would describe this effect on the reader as 'the pressure of the unfamiliar'.[48] Whatever life is felt in this narrative is supplied by the reader, and therein lies the relevance of my theme, for it is just this encounter that brings the reader to a point behind the mediating storyteller, lured to fill in this gap by the stylistic orchestrations of Joyce.

'Not to put too fine a point on it' (*U*, 614), the significance of this episode is that the reader's expectations are 'ambushed' (Joyce told Linati that the meaning of 'Eumaeus' was 'Ambush at home') by the otherness of the duplicitous language and the quiet *dénouement* of Bloom and Stephen's meeting.

The result is that the reader's expectations are jarred. Instead of certitude, the episode's narrational point of view offers only a partial truth, a kind of uncertainty the reader first fully encountered at least in 'Wandering Rocks', and perhaps in 'Aeolus', with the 'abrupt stylistic departure',[49] of its famous puzzling headings so unlike anything in the initial style of the first six episodes. The reader is left with a sense that any hope for a fixed style will be undermined. This hope for certitude is ambushed, and the gap between limited point of view and the reality behind it remains permanent. Indeed, as Marilyn French has shown throughout her superb book, '*Ulysses* is an epic of relativity'.[50] As the technique Joyce used for communication, style plays a crucial role and changes in style increase out attention on how various are the ways of viewing reality. Iser writes: 'Joyce wanted to bring about, if not actually overcome, the inadequacy of style as regards the presentation of reality, by constant changes of style, for only by showing up the relativity of each form could he expose the intangibility and expansibility of observable reality.'[51] The obvious implication of *Ulysses*' being written in numerous, varying styles is that 'the view expressed by each style is to be taken as only one possible facet of everyday reality',[52] and that no one perspective can offer a full purchase of the real. One might suggest that Joyce has prestructured just this meaning, through the arranger, so that the reader, to actualise it, has had to bring in tow all the formal expectations of the continously diminishing plot.

Rather than finding ourselves casting a calculating ironic eye over the events of the book, and thereby breaking loose from the hold of its pages, we discover that our engagement calls for our breaking free from our normal expectations of fiction. We recognise that the text invites the interpretation that style functions as an aspect of the book's meaning. 'Eumaeus' performs the complete acceptance of the inadequacy of language, of language as 'the vehicle of deception',[53] at just the time when the reader most hopes for a thematic resolution to this novel. It is a performance that leads the reader to a meaningful moment of 'poised ambiguity' (the phrase is Robert Alter's), at the episode's end. If the reader is of a Heideggerian persuasion, he may acknowledge at this point, as Robert Magliola says, that 'the text "originates" a new and unique epiphany of Being – an epiphany no other work can ever duplicate'.[54]

My assessment of the 'Eumaeus' episode reflects the renewed interest in the degree to which we are trying to become contemporaries of Joyce, as Ellmann first expressed the matter more than 25 years ago. Yet this interest has recently been characterised by interpretative moves that are seen to contrast markedly with the general interests of formalism sketched in Chapter 2. It is to the widening play of such interpretations that much Joyce criticism is heading, and I hope I have suggested as much by the recent scholarship I have drawn on to support my argument. To view the notion of epiphany as a faith in the ability of language to lay hold of or capture reality, and to experience as a reader 'Eumaeus's deflation of the dramatic climax, this 'extremely muted ingathering' of the two characters we have such vested interest in, is to recognise simultaneously the importance of the reader during the diminishing significance of character, and to know the magisterial power of Joyce in his refusal to give the reader certainty when *Ulysses* insists on our encountering the incertitude of the void.

5

Hermeneutic Otherness: 'A Feeling of Deflection from a Viable Centre' in Reading *A Severed Head*

> The skills involved in apprehending possibilities of perception from other centers of consciousness, for whom there are different patterns of salience, are integral to the creation and appreciation of literature. It is the centrality of this kind of perception that brings morality and literature together. For this is precisely what good literature achieves: the transcending of self, in the sense of the realisation and appreciation of genuinely 'other' centers of consciousness.[1]

I

> The strange is construed rather than explained; hermeneutic hesitation leads to a more positive awareness of otherness.[2]

The theme of epiphanic otherness discussed in the previous chapter emphasised the reader's experience of what might be called a seizure into the synchronic, a moment when the reader recognises, as the progress of the story diminishes, that the *effect* of the work can be a significant dimension of its meaning. It led us to the awareness that Joyce's stylistic teachniques renew our attention for and enable us to see freshly the otherness of reality as announced wholly, solely, by limited perspectives. In *The Political Unconscious*, Fredric Jameson calls this the effect of 'diachronic agitation',[3] and Geoffrey Hartman has described the experience as 'epiphanous resonance'[4] in *Criticism in the Wilderness*. Recent critical thought, I would suggest, has been wrestling with ways of understanding the act of reading when, in David Hoy's terms, it makes 'hermeneutics more "restless"'.[5] In my view, the tension within the idea of epiphany is that it may be seen to press towards the idea of archetype, that the 'whatness' showing forth must be some universal pattern; thus, one recalls that the paradigmatic example of the return to the 'mythic' stage for Northrop Frye is *Finnegans Wake*.

But I see the unique moment recognised by the act of reading pointing as well to hermeneutical considerations, especially when the issues of a second reading are taken into consideration. Vladimir Nabokov admits as much in his *Lectures on Literature* when he writes: 'Curiously enough, one cannot *read* a book; one can only reread it. A good reader, a major reader, an active and creative reader is a rereader.'[6] Structuralist emphases open the way to hermeneutical possibilities as the reader assumes a more constitutive role in our understanding of literature and its sense of otherness. To show the nature of this direction, and to bring this study to the form of closure it will admit, I shall now turn to a recent writer practised in the art of 'making strange' the literary universe: Iris Murdoch and a close rereading of her fifth novel, *A Severed Head*.

II

> Even 'I am tall' has a context.... Yet what can one do but try to lodge one's vision somehow inside this layered stuff of ironic sensibility, which, if I were a fictitious character, would be that much deeper and denser?
> Bradley Pearson, the central character and narrator of *The Black Prince*[7]

> The impenetrability of response exhibited by the fact that no [character] acts consistently as one might predict is a great surprise to the reader, and the repeated destructions of the reader's expectations serve Murdoch's purposes well.[8]

Robert Scholes is to my knowledge the first critic to recognise that *A Severed Head* can follow naturally from concerns and techniques expressed in *Ulysses*. In *Structuralism in Literature*, Scholes notes that the elements suggesting this continuity are structuralist in character. In his provocative last chapter, 'The Structuralist Imagination', Scholes includes structuralist discussion of Coleridge, *Ulysses* and *A Severed Head*. To point up the continuity between romanticism and structuralism, Scholes describes 'a shift from an atomistic and ontological view of language (individual words representing things in reality) to a view that is contextual and epistemological (combinations of words representing mental processes). The latter view... operates powerfully... in romantic thought in general.'[9] In contrast to Wordsworth's theory of language, Coleridge locates 'the distinction between rustic and educated language precisely at the point which divides the atomic from the structural properties of language. And he develops this view [when he relates] the "best part of language" not to external objects but to human mental processes.'[10]

Of Joyce's relation to structuralism, Scholes writes: 'For the later Joyce in particular – the Joyce of the last chapters of *Ulysses* and *Finnegans Wake* – was a man who had adapted an essentially structuralist view of the world.'[11] Such an adaptation may result in the 'collapse of individuated characterization' recognised in my argument in the preceding chapter. It is this collapse of character that Scholes believes links *A Severed Head* to *Ulysses*. I too hold that the threat of such collapse *is* thematised in both works, but I wish to argue at just this point the success of Murdoch in resisting this influence, engaging it rather through her narrative devices and compelling the reader to respond to it. Murdoch, in my view, succeeds precisely in her *not* illustrating this aspect of the structuralist imagination. One finds her awesomely accomplished in her effort to engage the reader hermeneutically precisely because of her success with character and her risky allegiance to a form of realism.

Thus, Scholes is led in his argument, for example, to insist that

> Iris Murdoch is a greater novelist than Sartre... not – as she might have hoped – because she has captured the 'absurd irreducible uniqueness' of people but because she has illustrated their rational similarity and relatedness. This is why the dominant motif of all her work has been not alienation but is opposite: love.[12]

This is a curious misreading of Murdoch, given the particular terms Scholes chooses to use. Murdoch is characteristically quite specific in her use of the word 'love', and she understands its meaning in a way dissimilar to that of Scholes. In 'The Sublime and the Good' she says:

> Love is the perception of individuals. Love is the extremely difficult realization that something other than oneself is real. Love, and so art and morals, is the discovery of reality.[13]

And when such momentous love is experienced by a character, all in life is indeed transformed. One example for the present must suffice, this from a woman in Murdoch's extraordinary novel, *The Book and the Brotherhood*:

> She had been re-created, given new being, new pure flesh, new lucid spirit. She could perceive the world at last, her eyes were cleared, her perceptions clarified, she had never seen such a vivid, coloured, detailed world, vast and complete as myth, yet full of tiny particular accidental entities placed in her way like divine toys. She had discovered breathing, breathing of the planet, of the universe, the movement of being into Being.[14]

If we focus on the intentionality of Murdoch's narrators in the telling of their tales – from *Under the Net* in 1954 to *The Philosopher's Pupil*[15] in 1983 – and on the various strategies they employ to engage their readers hermeneutically, we shall be able to affirm what structuralists have taught us about the role of the reader without forfeiting what our reading experience teaches us about the possibility of character. We can use our reading of *The Black Prince* as a propaedeutic into our understanding of *A Severed Head*, for the intentions of the fiction are made more explicit with the narrator of *The Black Prince*, Bradley Pearson, whereas with the telling told us by Martin Lynch-Gibbon, they are embedded in the narrative. With these intentions clarified, we can then describe the experience of the prepared mind in readings of *A Severed Head*.

Both stories are offered by means of Murdoch's use of male first-person flawed narrators. Both Martin and Bradley have moved out of their moribund initial state into a possibly freer world, and both tellings chart their developing sense of their spiritual progress. Both characters are pulled by unexpected personal encounters from stagnancy into novel, risky, perilous involvements in life. Both portray themselves as remarkably unlikable, unloving, ego-heavy personalities. Both experience a breakthrough because of unsolicited, surprising, cataclysmic experiences of love for a woman that wrenches them from their inauthentic existence.

Though *The Black Prince* offers multiple points of view through its forewords and postscripts, both novels employ irony to maximum advantage as a necessary device in the posture from which the telling is rendered. Both fictions are expressed by narrators casting themselves as naïvely entering the plot, without the benefit of hindsight, but Bradley Pearson is explicit about this technique of the double persona, whereas, in *A Severed Head*, Martin Lynch-Gibbon demands a more rigorous hermeneutic engagement from the reader, suggesting different interpretative moves in order for this crucial fact to be uncovered. Murdoch places tremendous weight on the significance of the reader's engagement with such narration. Time and again we feel reminded that here we have a novelist 'who is trying to get past mere reader-winning conventions'[16] in her effort to limn our limited complacent perceptions of reality. Because of such intentions, she is quite candid about them: many of us find ourselves confronting a Murdoch novel as – to use an interesting phrase of Edward Said's – an 'unwelcome cipher'.[17]

Much of my following argument depends on a technique adopted by Murdoch in both *The Black Prince* and the much earlier work, *A Severed Head*, a technique of autobiographical retrospection rare enough in the practice of modern fiction. The technical difference between the two tellers created by Murdoch is that in *The Black Prince*, the ageing novelist, Bradley Pearson, explicitly acknowledges his intent for the use and significance of the fictional devices described by him, whereas in *A Severed Head*, the reader must discover this intention of the teller through rereading. Here is Bradley Pearson's description, as he outlines it in the 'Foreword' to 'Bradley Pearson's Story':

> Although several years have now passed since the events recorded in this fable, I shall in telling it adopt the modern technique of narration, allowing the narrating consciousness to pass like a light along its series of present moments, aware of the past, unaware of what is to come. I shall, that is, inhabit my past self and, for the ordinary purposes of story-telling, speak only with the apprehensions of that time, a time in many ways so different from the present. So for example I shall say, 'I am fifty-eight years old,' as I then was. And I shall judge people, inadequately, perhaps even unjustly, as I then judged them, and not in the light of any later wisdom. That wisdom however, as I trust that I truly think it to be, will not be absent from the story. It will to some extent, in fact it must, 'irradiate' it. A work of art is as good as its creator. It cannot be more so. Nor, such as he in this case is, can it be less.[18]

Here we have a narrative presented by Bradley Pearson. This story (and the aforementioned 'Foreword') is enclosed by an 'Editor's Foreword' written by one 'P. Loxias', an unseen voice who functions as the editor (Bradley has entrusted him with the manuscripts of the novel in the prison they had shared for several years), and also by four 'Postscripts by Dramatis Personae' offered by significant characters in Bradley's story, in which they respond with their thoughts on the narrative after Bradley Pearson's death. I know of no other work by Murdoch that faces the question of form so directly, but she self-consciously wrestles with form versus the freedom of character in every act of creation, and it would be prudent to discuss Murdoch's declared intentions for the role of fiction in the modern world before we undertake a sustained description of the reader's hermeneutic engagement with Martin Lynch-Gibbon's telling.

III

> The experience of reading can liberate one from adaptations, prejudices, and predicaments of a lived praxis in that it compels one to a new perception of things. The horizon of expectations of literature... not only preserves actual experiences, but also anticipates unrealized possibility, broadens the limited space of social behavior for new desires, claims, and goals, and thereby opens paths of future experiences.[19]

> Art indeed, so far from being a playful diversion of the human race, is the place of its most fundamental insight, and the centre to which the more uncertain steps of metaphysics must constantly return.[20]

An understanding of *A Severed Head*, to begin with my fundamental claim, must be governed by the relationship between the work of fiction and the reader. This novel demands from the reader an encounter profitably considered as an intersection of the formalist literary critical tradition discussed above and those studies in religion and literature harbouring close association, as suggested by the epigraphs already cited and those included below, to dimensions of interpretation theory. Of the former, I simply mean to suggest the traditional American New Critical attitude of 'clerkly patience'[21] with the 'text itself',[22] together with the by now embattled presuppositions which this attitude entails; by the latter, I wish to note the possibility that much can occur liminally between the text and the consciousness of the reader. Iris Murdoch knows this (indeed, Elizabeth Dipple's accomplished study on Murdoch may be characterised in large measure as a species of reader-response criticism). Martin Lynch-Gibbon, the central character of the novel, knows this too, though for the reader this last fact is experienced only tacitly after a single reading (suggested by 'the feeling of deflection from a viable centre'[23] announced in this chapter's title). As the reader's mind works on the strategies of the text by way of a process of anticipation and retrospection, this tacit dimension discloses what might be resident within the 'appearance' of Martin's telling of his story.

And so this chapter will be concerned with those acts of interpretation leading to the realisation of a specific text. I intend the discussion to show that the element of irony may make a profound difference in one's posture of interpretation during the act of reading. I shall argue that the strategy of what I call 'implicative irony' can provide an adequate vehicle for prehensions of otherness.[24] To recall my own velleities for the reader's experience of literature first discussed in Chapter 1, I offer the following: the reader ought not to bypass hermeneutics, but if she does she runs the risk of making the rhetorical dimension of fiction the linchpin of the reader's understanding. I confess my increasing suspicion that the critical act poorly deployed will bully its way into making familiar that in the aesthetic experience which, if truly heard, cannot be familiarised (although this reference to the Russian formalists is explicit in such a remark, I would wager that probably my respect for John Crowe Ransom is surfacing here in this admission). When we are privileged to have a novelist in our midst like Murdoch, who takes extraordinary pains to bring the reader to a proximate recognition of this redoubtable 'otherness', then we might be well advised to reread a Murdoch novel carefully. This chapter, therefore, is in part the chronicling of my response, as reader, to the experience of being at first unwittingly implicated by a rather peculiar novel. This discussion will be an extended effort to ponder descriptively the hermeneutical experience brought to the reader's habitual way of seeing the world, a function of literature that brings to bear the connective link that may be experienced when the relationship between religion and literature functions at a significant pitch.

In assembling the world of the text by elucidating two potential meanings of Murdoch's novel, I am presuming that one potentiality can never realise the finished meaning of the text (such a presumption is tempered by the experience of such profoundly modern works as *Moby-Dick* and *Ulysses*, surely). Though *A Severed Head* has a measure of validity at both levels of reading presented, it is the second which I find more interesting, largely because upon a first reading the text's 'original negativity', as Hans Robert Jauss denotes it, 'is not made self-evident'.[25]

Iris Murdoch's fifth novel is a complex, carefully rendered narrative which, when understood in terms of who is telling the tale, may be seen to be one of her most successful endeavours. For the purposes of this chapter, it also allows serious engagement with crucial elements in the contemporary literary-critical enterprise. All that follows either leads towards or responds to a discussion of the central character and voice of *A Severed Head*. Because such a study requires an understanding of Murdoch's repetoire, we begin with a consideration of her programme of aesthetics, especially with regard to what she hopes fictional charactersation can accomplish. This will be followed by an examination of the convention of point-of-view and its impact on Martin's own ability to relate his story, and then a discussion of the ironic nature of narrative itself as it relates to the reality suggested thematically and structurally in the novel. A major point to be argued is that one may speak meaningfully about the 'virtuality' of a literary work, understanding 'virtuality' to be, as Iser posits, the imprecise though dynamic region between the artistic and aesthetic poles of a literary work. Iser speaks of this region as the 'convergence of the text and reader',[26] and also as 'the coming together of text and imagination',[27] during the process of mutual implication. I shall develop this later aspect once the discussion is well along.

Murdoch has written, in her exacting, precise manner, of the task on which novelists must, in this post-Romantic era, focus their energies: 'Through literature we can rediscover a sense of the density of our lives.'[28] She says of humanity's condition; 'We no longer see man against a background of values, of realities, which transcend him. For the hard idea of truth we have substituted a facile idea of sincerity.[29] 'We need to be enabled... to picture, in a non-metaphysical, non-totalitarian, and non-religious sense, the transcendence of reality.... We need to return from the self-centered concept of sincerity to the other-centered concept of truth.'[30] Just so, it is the interpretation of the reader's encounter with this transcending sense of 'otherness' that figures significantly in the present study. The use of the word 'return' is the above quote indicates that, in Murdoch's view, the representation of characters in prose fiction as opaque, eccentric – in a word, as 'other' – has occurred before. She looks to Dickens, George Eliot, Tolstoy and Jane Austen as successful examples of novelists who could create characters seemingly divorced from the authors' personalities. In an interview with Frank Kermode, Murdoch admits:

> One isn't good enough at creating character.... I start off – hoping every time that this is going to happen and that a lot of people who are not me are going to come into existence in some wonderful way. Yet often it turns out in the end that something about the structure of the work itself, the myth as it were of the work, has drawn all these people into a sort of spiral, or into a kind of form which ultimately is the form of one's own mind.[31]

To me such statements suggest that fictive apprehensions of otherness are moments which signal to our imaginations that all is *not* a figment of the mind, that the real does exist beyond our fabulations. Put another way, our primitive awareness comports to the feeling of being in the world, not to the notion of constructing a world. To come to terms with this sense of real otherness which is lodged in that which is transcendent of the perceiving mind – Murdoch asks no less than this of her reader. We could accordingly characterise Murdoch's philosophy as neo-realist. Throughout Murdoch's writings, the emphasis on our need to see clearly our situation is sustained.

Thus, the necessary yet elusive project of creating character participates in the larger scheme of art's difficult function. Although many critics find themselves drawn to Murdoch's theoretical statements with a sense of 'baffled piety',[32] one surely feels the verve, the punch, the unabashed conviction of Murdoch's view when she writes unequivocally:

> Good art, unlike bad art, unlike 'happenings', is something preeminently outside us and resistant to our consciousness. We surrender ourselves to its *authority* with a love which is unpossessive and unselfish. Art shows us the only sense in which the permanent and incorruptible is compatible with the transient; and whether representational or not it reveals to us aspects of our

world which our ordinary dull dream-consciousness is unable to see. Art pierces the veil and gives sense to the notion of a reality which lies beyond appearance; it exhibits virtue in its true guise in the context of death and chance.[33]

And so Murdoch holds that ours is a late and anxious time. She writes for and about those of us who, 'as contemporaries...are late-born, with only an educated apprehension of once workable connections through devices like art, myth or history',[34] as Dipple so strikingly phrases it. People need to confront their bits of reality which, when assembled, say, in the formulations of art, tell them that truth is no longer absolute and must be approached and known on a personal level. One is no longer able to believe in a universe characterised by teleological unity, says Murdoch, and so one must accept items of the inexplicable. Now, the problem with the relativisation of truth has been embodied in the recent fiction of many other writers, to be sure; it may be found readily in fictively deceptive techniques as various as those of Robert Coover and John Fowles. But beyond the pale of this prevalent aspect of contemporary writing, it should be noted that Murdoch's awareness of and preservation of the necessity for characterisation limns the sense of otherness that necessarily obtains for the reader as he realises such characterisation.

In view of the issue of truth experienced on a personal, individual plane, the central tension of *A Severed Head* is the delicate poising required between the integral portrayal of the myth of the severed head – as a developing symbol for the emotional and mysterious mythological dimension of human experience – and the degree to which the characters, in their unmitigated individuality, are free from the formalising impulse of fiction itself. Are the characters merely pawns, illustrations formally strung together to promote the allegorical 'message' of the myth? Or does the mythic significance arise *from* the interactions of these various characters in their various moments of fictive life? If the form of the book is built around the myth, Murdoch believes the myth will swallow any tolerance for the 'otherness of other persons', and thus will annul the possibility (given this moral view of reality) of realising greater degrees of love. Frank Baldanza notes:

> Miss Murdoch maintains that it is precisely in this experience of the sublime – in which the reason is in part defeated, but not

humbled – that man will find his greatest fulfillment. This poses special problems for the artist, since art is required to have form; but it must never find form by limiting freedom, eccentricity, and independence of the persons treated in the novel.[35]

The novel must somehow achieve a form that yet renders the contingent shapelessness of actual life. What the novel form requires, then, is an adequate balance.

Reality transcends the individual – this awareness may precede or coincide with one's own ability genuinely to love another being. Murdoch's work centres upon the imaginative portrayal of fictive consciousness approaching, in some degree of freedom, the experience of love. Of course, the freedom to engage in transcending reality will always be a matter of degree (thus, the title of A.S. Byatt's well-known book, *Degrees of Freedom*), for the sense of total love in Murdoch's world necessarily would be illusory. Murdoch frequently renders this sense in the guise of some form of enchantment. Sharon Kaehele and Howard German emphasize that the 'higher type of freedom which Miss Murdoch calls for is an indefinitely extended capacity to imagine the being of others; freedom of this sort is a tragic freedom because extending such attention to other individuals leads inevitably to a recognition of the unalterable and irreconcilable differences among individuals'.[36]

I stated earlier that a thorough re-reading of *A Severed Head* yields the suggestion that there are two ways to approach an understanding of the central character, Martin Lynch-Gibbon, the second of which emerges embodying a much more complex irony. I shall now discuss, with relevant support from the text, both approaches in detail.

IV

> Irony presents a human conflict which ... is unsatisfactory and incomplete unless we see in it a significance beyond itself.... What that significance is, irony does not say: it leaves that question up to the reader.[37]

The efficacy of a literary text is brought about by the apparent evocation and subsequent negation of the familiar. What at first seemed to be an affirmation of our assumptions leads to our own rejection of them, thus tending to prepare us for a re-orientation. And it is only when we have outstripped our preconceptions and left the shelter of the familiar that we are in a position to gather in new experience.[38]

A Severed Head is about Martin's struggle to understand the 'nightmare' into which he feels he has been 'plunged'. It is an account in which the reader is invited to watch Martin slowly come to a degree of mature awareness about the reality that lies beyond the drawing-room society in which he, at the beginning of the story, is thoroughly ensconced. In Murdochian terms, his moral maturation is traced through a series of episodes which, in turn, illustrate his failure to explain rationally his strange experiences.

But degress of irony obtrude from the structural core of the story, and the reader must attempt to understand how irony functions in characterising Martin. A discussion of the phenomenon of irony may be found in the excellent study by Robert Scholes and Robert Kellogg, *The Nature of Narrative*:

> By definition narrative art requires a story and a storyteller. In the relationship between the teller and the tale, and that other relationship between the teller and the audience, lies the essence of narrative art. The narrative situation is thus ineluctably ironical. Irony is always the result of a disparity of understanding. In any situation in which one person knows or perceives more – or less – than another, irony must be either actually or potentially present. In any example of narrative art there are, broadly speaking, three points of view – those of the characters, the narrator, and the audience. As narrative becomes more sophisticated, a fourth point of view is the clear distinction between the narrator and the author. Narrative irony is a function of disparity among these three or four viewpoints.[39]

And it is point of view that controls this irony:

> In the eye-witness form of narration, considerations of character are intimately related to considerations of point of view. To the extent that the narrator is characterized he will dominate the narrative, taking precedence over event and situation. [The device of the unreliable eye-witness] lends an especially ironical cast to an entire narrative, laying on the reader a special burden of enjoy-

able ratiocination, as he seeks to understand what the character telling the story cannot himself comprehend. Because of its intellectual possibilities, this has become a favourite device in didactic and satiric narratives.[40]

At the level at which I am now considering it, *A Severed Head* may be seen, formally, as a comedy satirically presented. What quickens the story from moment to moment is the ironic tension that endures within and through Martin, and ultimately rests in the fabricating pen of Murdoch herself. Martin is unreliable to the degree that he is a fallible narrator. Such a 'type' has been defined by M. H. Abrams as

> the teller of the story [as] himself a participant in it but, although he may be neither foolish nor demented, nevertheless [manifesting] a failure of insight, viewing and appraising his own motives, and the motives and actions of other characters, through the distorting perspective of his prejudices and private interests.[41]

Iris Murdoch, in this specific sense of being the author-narrator, is felt on every page to be the creative force without which nothing could come into being. I would point to such examples as the particularities of detail, the wit and irony the reader sees (qualities which the reader knows simultaneously Martin does not see), the carefully planted central symbolism which blooms nicely into a concise statement by Honor Klein near the end of the novel, and the balanced geometric composition of clandestine and revealed relationships which fold and unfold time and again.

To elaborate on this vital concept: an 'ironic gap' emerges at every moment when the reader senses that more is present in a given bit of narrative than Martin seems to be aware of. Such gaps, Iser claims, function for the reader as spurs to interaction with the text. With his characteristic historic bent, Martin presumes to be telling, from his view of the situation, about the nightmare into which he was 'plunged'. But the reader is in league with Murdoch at every moment when imaginative style leaps 'beyond' Martin's sensibility, beyond what the reader at this point determines to be Martin's intentionality. Such interaction on the reader's part effects a unity of meaning which owes final allegiance to the novel's artistic impact, and *not* to Martin's sincerity.

Thus, the fact that Martin mentions all the key themes and all central characters of the book in the first chapter betrays the reality that it is Murdoch pulling the strings of the story and not, as Martin supposes, himself. This is ironic, and it enlivens the narrative flow from page to page. I shall now turn to several concrete examples which support this *first level of reading*.

The novel ironically begins with a note of assumed sureness: Martin is so distanced from reality that he can feel virtuous about his willed deception of his wife Antonia (regarding his affair with Georgie Hands). The book ends with a felt sense of risk and uncertainty about Martin's future with Honor Klein. Essentially, Martin is left at the point of either becoming or not becoming a real person, *and the reader is left wondering to what degree Martin has actually changed, if at all*.

Of course, this is certainly not where Martin is found at the beginning. Having just returned from a 'moment of great peace' in Georgie's 'subterranean place, remote, enclosed, hidden', the reader is privy to Martin's complacent thoughts:

> [I] thought myself, I dare say, the luckiest of men. Indeed at the moment I was happy with an idle, thoughtless happiness which was never to come, with that particular quality of degenerate innocence, ever in my life again. (*SH*, 24)[42]

As Martin puts it, he is 'still in the slow old world'. After Antonia's revelation of her love and desired marriage to Palmer Anderson (her psychoanalyst), all in Martin's universe begins to go awry: 'I had a sense of miserable confusion and of things having utterly escaped my control' (*SH*, 30). 'The familiar world of ways and objects within which I had lived for so long received me no more' (*SH*, 37). 'The things in it no longer cohered' (*SH*, 38). 'It was ironical...that a week ago I had seemed in secure possession of two women; now I was likely to be in possession of neither...as I speculated and wondered about what exactly Georgie *would* expect, it occurred to me how little, after all, I knew her' (*SH*, 39). A while later Martin writes in a letter to Georgie: 'I don't altogether know myself. Indeed, I feel scarcely sane and nothing seems solid any longer or real for the present' (*SH*, 54).

Such ruminations fill the first quarter of the novel. Martin, because of exterior events, is forced to realise how little control he actually has over other people; a gnawing pain grows within that will remind him of the reality of his separateness throughout the

Hermeneutic Otherness

course of the book. Yet, although he has apparently reflected much along the philosophical lines one expects of a Murdochian narrator, Martin is far from possessing a free capacity to love the 'otherness of other people'. Examples abound illustrating Martin's sexist chauvinism, his consitutional inability to receive and be informed by the 'otherness' of the women he encounters and labours to appropriate for his own ends. For example, he can state that he now views Antonia as a 'separate person and no longer a part of myself' (*SH*, 59). He also realises how much he needs the comfort, the cushioning, of Georgie: 'The pressure upon me of Georgie's needs, any requirement that I should now imagine *her* situation, would be intolerable, and I felt sick at the thought. Yet I did want to see her. I wanted consolation, I wanted love, I wanted, to save me, some colossal and powerful love such as I had never known before' (*SH*, 63). This is both comic and ironic because it is exactly at this moment when Honor's train arrives, together with all the horror, confusion, mess and muddle that ensue.

The counterpoising which, throughout the remainder of the novel, casts significant meaning on Martin's struggle with reality is the mythic presence of Honor. It is she who, embodying the Murdochian sensibility, lurks behind any of Martin's pretensions and illusions. The effect, of course, is a developing emphasis on Martins' habitual selecting of inauthentic actions.

The first extended conversation between Honor and Martin is a necessary example. Honor tries to make Martin face the fact that Antonia and Palmer are enchanted with their relationship. In three of her comments it is seen that the situation demands that Martin not be so soft: 'They are both persons with a great capacity for self-deception' (*SH*, 75); 'By gentleness you only spare yourself and prolong this enchantment of untruth which they have woven about themselves and about you too' (*SH*, 76); 'All I say is that only lies and evil come form letting people off' (*SH*, 77).

After this strange and challenging interview, Martin retreats to the illusory safety of Georgie, and one feels immediately how different Georgie and Honor are in Martin's view of things: 'I could have wept with relief. I loved her so much at that moment that I nearly knelt down then and there and proposed. I kissed her hands humbly. "Yes, I am in a fix," I said, "but you'll be kind to me, won't you? You'll let me off?"' (*SH*, 78). Because Martin allows himself the illusion of gentleness with Georgie, he can think: 'Here at last I was free' (*SH*, 80).

But Georgie intrudes: 'As for breaking down the doubleness, we can't really do that until we stop telling lies.' Martin, characteristically, wishes to withdraw from such an opening into reality: 'I didn't want this argument.' Georgie, it is clear, has echoed, exactly, Honor's point. Such reverberations of Honor's presentation of reality emphasise her relevance thematically, and subconsciously, for the reader, perhaps her grounding, mythic presence.

By Chapter 11 we read the following beginning: 'The next thing was that Georgie was not at her place.' The first four words are unique and odd, yet they suggest the degree to which Martin views his immersion into the events surrounding him. He feels a developing consequential inevitability that is making it more difficult to 'be let off'. Because Martin hates and fears this agonising divorce from his 'old world', he loses himself in whiskey, or in the illusion of control over Georgie ('[I] felt confident of bringing her around fairly easily'), or seeks out – as was metioned above – gentleness and comfort from those two, Antonia and Palmer, who are as far from reality as he is: 'At least here were people who could be gentle with me' (*SH*, 89). But even this expectation is ironic, for when he visits he sees immediately that they know of his secret affair with Georgie. Rational and controlled, Palmer and Antonia insist on understanding Martin's behaviour as logically as a true explanation of things might allow. The reader receives another subtle clue that perhaps Martin has changed or matured somewhat, for inchoately Martin feels: 'Understanding was out of the question; and indeed how passionately, just then, I did not want to be understood' (*SH*, 93).

Seeing Georgie again, Martin discovers that she had revealed everything to Honor Klein. Honor had subsequently revealed all to Antonia. Incredulous that Georgie could commit such a *faux pas*, he asks, 'Why?' and Georgie responds, 'Because it was impossible to lie to her' (*SH*, 100).

On New Year's Eve, Martin meets Honor again at Palmer's house, in the dining room. When Martin says that she believes 'in the dark gods', Honor unexpectedly replies, 'I believe in people.'

Martin then has a series of transcending experiences which signal, for himself and for the reader, a definite change in his perception of the world that rests beyond his being. Or, in other words, these experiences occur at Martin's felt moments of freedom beyond his self. He is slowly cast into the night where 'one is aware of other galaxies'.

Hermeneutic Otherness

The first instance arises down in the bleak, cavernous cellar in Palmer's house. As Martin suddenly encounters Honor, he feels the following:

> My heart knocked still, and for a moment I had the strange experience of seeming to stand outside and see myself, a tall stooping figure, my coat collar turned up, my hair wild, my eyes staring, and the wine half spilt. I found it difficult to speak.
> [Honor's] eyes opened with a little ironical light.   (*SH*, 133)

Later, tormented about his violent fight with Honor in the cellar, Martin walks along the Thames:

> I felt on the whole a thorough nausea about recent events.... [T]here were times when I wondered whether my love for Georgie was strong enough to support the sheer weight of mess and muddle under which it now laboured.   (*SH*, 145)

'Mess and muddle' is a favourite phrase used by Murdoch to describe how contingent and inexplicable life really is. At this moment Martin has his second experience. It is an epiphany which reveals the sheer facticity, **the unmitigated otherness of the real beyond the self, expressed here by** his encounter with a glowing telephone box:

> I looked at the telephone box; and as I looked it seemed to take on a strange sudden glory, such as is said to invest the meanest object in the eyes of those who claim to experience the proof of the existence of God *e contingentia mundi*.... Very dimly and distantly, but hugely, it began to dawn upon me what the nature of my ailment was. It was something new and something, as I even at once apprehended, terrible.... It was the sort of night when one knows of other galaxies. When the idea came to me that I was desperately, irrevocably, agonizingly in love with Honor Klein it seemed at first to shed a great light.   (*SH*, 149–50)

Then, thinking over the possible reasons why he feels cataclysmically chosen to love Honor, Martin reflects:

> There had been no moment when I reassessed her character, noticed new qualities or passed less harsh judgments on the old

ones: which seemed to imply that I now loved her for the same
things for which I had previously disliked her.... [I]t was in truth
a monstrous love such as I had never experienced before, a love
out of such depths of self as monsters live in. A love devoid of
tenderness and humour, a love practically devoid of personality.
(*SH*, 152)

Overwhelmed by this force, Martin goes to Cambridge to see
Honor. The measure of his enchantment is seen in the contrast
between his dream of her as 'free, as alone, as waiting in her
still slumbering consciousness for me, reserved, separate, sacred',
and the shocking discovery that she is in bed with her brother,
Palmer.

A later inverview with Honor provides the central discussion
about how she, in Martin's view of things, is 'a terrible object of fascination', in fact, a 'severed head such as primitive tribes and old
alchemists used to use' to receive prophetic knowledge.

Undaunted by her remark that 'as real people we do not exist for
each other', Martin finally arrives at his personal either/or:

[E]ither I would lose Honor, in which case all would be as before,
or else, *per impossible*, I would gain her, and this would create a
new heaven and a new earth and the utter sweeping away of all
former things. I would be a new person; and if she were relent-
lessly to draw me I would come to her even if I had to wade
through blood. (*SH*, 225)

Martin, it may now be seen, has slowly entered this strange reality (represented by Honor Klein) throughout the book. Near its ending, the novel apocalyptically refers frequently to 'a new era' and 'a
new beginning', which Martin desperately expects in life. What is
'new' is the ongoing interim in which Martin asks all his questions
about why he has lost tidy control of his conventional life.

Chapter 30, the last of the novel, begins with something like the
estranged tone Meursault allows himself at the beginning of *The
Stranger*. An unrhythmic, indifferent and detached narrative is
found at this juncture. Martin sounds tired of the whole business,
having arrived home after secretively seeing Palmer, Georgie and
Honor prepare to board a plane. He does not know if he is hot or
otherwise, cannot remember if it has rained, and looks vaguely
about for some biscuits:

Of course I was still in a shocked state. I noticed my trembling hand, a tendency to shiver, a chattering of the teeth.

It was after all the first moment of some entirely new era. I supposed I would survive.... There has been a drama, there had been some characters, but now everyone else was dead and only in me a memory remained of what had been; and perhaps mercifully that memory too would fade, as in some crazed old prisoner who cannot recall his sufferings and not even know that he has been released. I attempted, as the pain increased, to cover it with a haze of consciousness, making myself, through some general chatter about my condition, anonymous and so not really suffering. But the sharp truth would not be denied and I became silent in the end and became myself in the knowledge of my unique loss. (*SH*, 244)

And then, surprisingly, Honor shows up, this time saying: 'I haven't come *to* torment you.' And Martin notices that 'there was an ironical lightness in her gaze'. This ironical look and smile remain until the end of the book, when Martin sees it 'now softening at last out of irony', as he realises that they will have equal footing in a chancy future, devoid of guarantees. Martin asks a series of questions about the prospects of this future together, and to each she merely responds with her ironical look or smile of silence. It is, then, irony itself that answers Martin's queries, and he makes note of this ironical, 'faint, stiff', 'deepened', 'narrow level', 'bright' smile twelve times in four pages. *Honor refuses to utter prophecies to which Martin might cling*:

> As she still would not speak, I said, 'Could we be happy?'
> She said, 'This has nothing to do with happiness, nothing whatever.'
> That was true. I took in the promise of her words. I said, 'I wonder if I shall survive it.'
> She said, smiling splendidly, 'You must take your chance!'
> I gave her back the bright light of her smile, now softening at last out of irony. 'So must you, my dear!'

This statement, bringing the novel to a close, brings Honor, at least momentarily for Martin, fully into human view. I now turn to a second reading, which raises an altogether different structure of possibility for the reader during his experience of this text.

V

> It might seem as though ironic naturalization makes more grandiose claims than the things which it deflates. At the moment when we propose that a text means something other than what it appears to say we introduce, as hermeneutic devices which are supposed to lead us to the truth of the text, models which are based on our expectations about the text and the world. Irony, the cynic might say, is the ultimate form of recuperation and naturalization, whereby we ensure that the text says only what we want to hear. We reduce the strange or incongruous, or even attitudes with which we disagree, by calling them ironic and making them confirm rather than abuse our expectations.[43]
>
> Meaning is a continual shuttling back and forth between the language of the work and a network of contexts which are not *in* the work but are essential for its realization.[44]

From the discussion presented thus far, it might be supposed that *A Severed Head* in its entirety poses exactly this for Martin: one cannot get beyond a 'maybe' to the locked surety of a rationally ordered life in one's future. Absolute truths cannot be found beyond the self or in the self. But to attempt a relationship of love with another human being engages a person in the highest degree of freedom possible, and in so doing increases his contact with reality. The reader might tend to feel cautious in assuming that Martin has, indeed, arrived at such a consciousness of reality as embraced by Honor and embodied in the philosophical ruminations of Bradley Pearson and the essays of Murdoch, especially when recalling that Murdoch herself 'has described her novels as pilgrimages from illusion towards reality, [and] also pointed out that "reality" as such is never arrived at in the books, any more than it is in life'.[45] Although it appears that the book ends ambiguously at this crucial moment in Martin's life, it is here the second, deeper structural irony of the book arises. The reader is brought to such a pass that he gains a different kind of consciousness of his entanglement with the text; he therefore reads the text again, and necessarily involves himself at a different level in his effort to actualise the ambiguity. The reader is induced, as Iser would have it, to 'familiarize the unfamiliar'.[46] Murdoch has sought to make Martin a demythicised Honor, and the remainder of this chapter will attempt to clarify why the novel successfully suggests such a possibility, and why the reader necessarily finds himself being implicated, mutually, actively, *with* the text, rather than having his personality 'handed over' (as the Geneva critics would urge) *to* the text. Both the interpreter and the interpreted, by way of the process of reading, are mutually implicated.

It is only by activating the reader's imagination that Martin can hope to involve the reader and so realise the intentions of his text/account. This experience of mutual implication is adequately addressed by Iser's epistemology:

> Thus we have the apparently paradoxical situation in which the reader is forced to reveal aspects of himself in order to experience a reality which is different from his own. The impact this reality makes on him will depend largely on the extent to which he himself actively provides the unwritten part of the text, and yet in supplying all the missing links, he must think in terms of experiences different from his own; indeed, it is only by leaving behind the familiar world of his own experience that the reader can truly participate in the adventure the literary text offers him.[47]

The ultimate signification the reader has of Martin's progression in meeting reality as it exits (or as Murdoch believes it to exist) is Martin's impulse, his desire to write his own 'story', the story present in the form of *A Severed Head*. Any lifeless, uninvolved caricature of himself as protrayed within the novel must always be viewed against the fact that, at present – 'present' being the time of the act of reading the book – Martin, a fictional character, is seeking, or engaged in, an imaginative encounter with the world beyond himself. We, the readers, in turn bring Martin to life by *our* leap into Murdoch's fictional world. It is during the time of this leap, of this reading, and the space it occupies, when the literary work 'happens', that the potential work is actualised. At this level Martin may be viewed as someone other than a 'fallible narrator', other than the limited character which the first half of this chapter has considered. As Scholes and Kellogg suggest: '[T]o the extent that the narrating character is differentiated from the author one ironic gap opens up, and to the extent that the narrating character is differentiated from himself as participant in events another gap appears.'[48]

It is my conviction that an ironic atmosphere expands the capacity for narrative meaning, the reader's participation in this dynamic meaning and, in effect, with regard to characterisation, 'blurs' the reader's ability to categorise into types and absolutes. *The reader is enjoined to learn, ironically, exactly what Martin is asked to learn.* The reader discovers that this text before us is not a closed 'thing' or 'object' to be observed, but rather an open-ended, dynamic event wherein, by virtue of experiencing the text's indeterminacy, the reader is engaged to formulate the intention beyond the selection of the repertoire's familiar components. Instead of one answer, one definitive meaning to this novel, one must be satisfied with the suggestion of many meanings. It is the reader's encounter with the relativisation of truth, as it is bodied forth by this hint of many meanings, which suggests this novel's post-modern quality. But the same might be said, for example, of Conrad's *Heart of Darkness*[49], or of the ending of John Fowles's *The Magus*, or of the three endings offered in *The French Lieutenant's Woman*. I wish to show, in the following discussion, that it is not merely in the deception of an unresolved ending that one finds multiple layers of meaning.

It may be noted that what moves the narrative of *A Severed Head*, primarily, is not the exposure of unexpected clandestine relationships (measured by Martin's renewable surprise and horror), but the promised of teleological resolution which pulls the reader, from page to page, to a final unveiling of just what this irony is measured *against*. Yet, the final surprise for the reader, as intially it must have been for Martin, is that, although there is a structural resolution in the novel's classically formed ending, the answer is kept only to Murdoch herself. In other words, the final answer is that there is *not* any final answer, but merely the presentation of Martin's ironic sensibility.

Because Martin's account ends ambiguously, and yet ends with his sincere intentions to tell it as it truly happened, the reader earns the sense that perhaps Martin wrote this 'telling' as an effort of personal ratiocination, as a method of approaching self-discovery. I have already viewed examples of his attempts to solve rationally or explain away his muddied situation. Murdoch suggests much the same 'method' in *The Sovereignty of Good*:

> Herein we find the remarkable redemption of our tendency to conceal death and chance by the invention of forms. Any story which we tell ourselves consoles us since it imposes pattern upon

something which might otherwise seem intolerably chancy or incomplete. It is the role of tragedy, and also of comedy, and of painting to show us suffering without a thrill and death without consolation. Or if there is any consolation it is the austere consolation of a beauty which teaches that nothing in life is of value except the attempt to be virtuous.[50]

It would be well, in order to understand the presence of the second, deeper degree of irony (which I shall call 'implicative irony'), to review certain vital instances in the novel where one may uncover the character Martin, created by Murdoch, conscious of himself as a writer of his own story.

Chapter 1 is nearly all narration such as the reader will discover throughout the rest of the book. Martin is immediately engaged in the telling of events, without any 'distanced', withdrawn explanation of himself as a writer. The only statement with a hint of the teller's being at one remove from his account is an example I have discussed before: Georgie's 'room seemed a subterranean place, remote, enclosed, hidden. It was for me a moment of great peace. I did not know then that it would be the last moment of peace, the end of the old innocent world, the final moment before I was plunged into the nightmare of which the ensuing pages tell the story' (*SH*, 12).

Chapter 2 backs up a bit, dealing largely with background history of the events already under way in Chapter 1. This narrative hiatus allows Martin to reveal self-consciously some important feelings about himself as the writer of the story: 'I seem to have started here upon some general explanation of myself, and it may be as well to continue this before I plunge into a narrative of events which may, once under way, offer few opportunities for meditation. My name, as you will have gathered...' (*SH*, 15). Martin is aware of an audience ('you'), and the audience's task of making sense of the story as it progresses (a process of interpretation that Robert Scholes reminds us Poe termed 'ratiocination'[51]). The passage also suggests that Martin has some sense of the internal power, the flow, of the story qua story: 'To describe one's character is difficult and not necessarily illuminating. The story which follows will reveal, whether I will or no, what sort of person I am' (*SH*, 15). Again, Martin here hints of the reliability (or what might be termed the 'thrust of truth') and trust one might feel about the ensuing narrative.

Also, by this time the sense has been built up (a sense intended by Martin?) that he has not written further than the point at which the audience is now reading: 'A word about Palmer is necessary; and this I find difficult. The pages that follow will show how and why my feelings on the subject of Palmer are mixed one. I shall only try now to describe him as I saw him at the start, before I knew certain crucial facts about him, and when I was more than a little "carried away"' (*SH*, 19). Such a passage advances the possibility that Martin has some definite notion of how to get the story rolling. He expresses confidence about the degree to which the pages of his account will be mimetically true – at least with regard to Palmer. This paragraph also indicates Martin's sense of control and proportion; namely, he thinks it better to begin at the beginning, with the suggestion of 'more to come', which helps the reader to push on, to expect development and a resolution of the story in later pages. The phrase quoted above, 'carried away', perhaps Martin's term for 'enchanted' – in this instance, of course, referring to homosexual impulses – is used in a definite past tense: Martin, as he writes this account after having experienced the story's events, no longer views himself as he once was. Though the sensibility expressed here by Martin may be less sophisticated in the techniques of narrative, we are briefly reminded of the narrative posture explicitly adopted by Bradley Pearson near his beginning of *The Black Prince*.

The reader's crucial ratiocinative task is to discern, if possible, to what degree the ironic gap (most open at the outset of his reading) between the 'implied author' and the narrating character, Martin, has closed. By 'implied author' I mean all the extratextual notions of Murdoch's repertoire that the reader brings to any single work. To be definite this, a central issue of this chapter: the aforesaid task is one of reconstruction. The degree to which the reader is compelled to reconstruct the narrative's surface, or literal, presentation, in order to arrive at the region of Murdoch's enverbalised consciousness, is the degree to which the book is rhetorically ironic. If (it is presumed) one can arrive at the level of Murdoch's platform as it is resident within the text – and Geneva critics insist that the critic can make such an effort – one's understanding of Martin's telling should clarify the ambiguities present at the level of the literal reading. Such reformulation, as Wayne Booth delineates the process in *The Rhetoric of Irony*, would lead the reader, in the present instance, to a local, covert irony.[52]

Hermeneutic Otherness 111

Yet a most subtle irony arises when the reader sees that he (ironically!) is so entangled that he, quite like Martin, *needs* to get hold of firmer footing. Both the reader and Martin are mutually implicated: it could not be otherwise, for it is the nature of this kind of literary work to *function* in this way when experienced at this implicatively ironic level.

The very nature of first-person narrative may provide the natural expectation of a definite resolution of events (that is, plot). Thus, Martin, one gathers, will end his account when he has come 'to terms with himself and realizes his nature'. Else why has Murdoch put this character through such trials? The reader has been led along to Martin's 'either/or' stated above. If Honor had not returned, one could accept Martin's own belief that he would sooner or later return to his own form of inauthentic living. I have noted that the book ends with a series of questions which the reader, along with Martin, feels justified to pose – particularly: '*can* (or will) Martin come to terms with Honor/Murdoch's view of reality?' But this, co-instantenously, is countered by another question: '*has* Martin come to terms with Honor/Murdoch's view of reality?' The latter arises from the impact of rhetorical irony, for it is a question between Murdoch and the reader, and not between the reader and Martin. The book presents both questions; the reader cannot ask both at the same time but, through efforts of reconstruction, may be led from the first to the second as soon as he or she begins exploring the evident fact that *A Severed Head* is a re-telling, namely, Martin's personal answer to the first question.

Now it must be recalled that Martin has been, by choice, an historian when not occupied with his inherited wine trade; he tells us of his publications on history. The reader also knows of Martin's awareness that what follows in his account of his story may offer a meaning that he feels is beyond himself, or at least 'other' than what he can intend, or see, in it. He may think he can only offer a sequential (that is, historical), accurate narration of events. Thus, the artistic meaning leaps beyond, or transcends, Martin's rational sensibility, and is, from his point of view, one sees, ironical. In his study, *Animate Illusions*, Harold Toliver comments: 'where history writing seeks to lay bare the event and the cause as distinctly as possible, the novel renders the process of discovery itself and suggests that it is not merely the reader's but is inherent in the enigmas the work seeks to clarify'.[53] So the reader may ask, 'does Martin know this?' Does he intend to lead 'you' into the expectation of a coherent ending, which Martin knows will not happen? Toliver continues:

> Whether or not the reactive witness is explicitly present within the work... the dramatic coherence of fiction assumes the presence somewhere of a knowing centre before which the material of the story is placed in a certain sequence and timing that gives it the coloration of dramatic discovery. Whereas historical narration seeks for coherence largely in the subject itself, or in general statements about it, and is forced to acknowledge frequently its partial success, fiction locates it in a controlled epistemological, dramatic process over which the art work has absolute control.[54]

The reader is led to wonder if, after all, Martin is *himself* being ironical. But then one would be led to suspect everything he says, and one would end up with no firm footing, but a piling of irony upon irony. This would be, of course, the kind of situation which is realised in many forms of post-modern fiction. If, without ironic intention, Martin is seeking historical accuracy, then the fact that his account appears as a novel is ironic from his view of things. One feels one is now on Murdoch's side of the fence, and can therefore accept the following quirk in Martin's presentation of events: before he recounts his violent, physical encounter with Honor on the cellar floor, he writes: 'What happened next may seem a little improbable, but the reader must just believe me that it did occur' (*SH*, 134). This statement focuses on Martin's awareness of the reader's struggle with the incredible. It also reinforces Martin's attempt to record events as they actually happened, and here asks of the reader the same leap into reality that Honor asks of Martin. The general flow is broken by a moment of raw incredulity, or the awareness that what is presently detailed might appear so. In this view, the reader can interpret the quote to be a *Murdochian* twist on the reader's expectations, and not a device designed by Martin.

But perhaps Martin deliberately intended to delineate his autobiography by rendering his new-found reality in a mythic mode. Such an interpretation, at least, suggests to what degree he has changed because of Honor. One critic, to my knowledge, has carried this aspect of the reality of Martin as a character to this extent, holding to the belief that Martin, indeed, writes his own story, and that this fact is of thematic concern central to the understanding of the novel (and not merely a structural device of 'first-person' eye-witness narration employed to get the story told). This is how Alice Kenny regards the matter: 'It is highly significant to historians as well as to students of literature that Martin Lynch-Gibbon's reading of mythology led directly to the composition of *A Severed Head* itself — a monographic history of human relationships, including both criticism of and expansion upon currently-accepted approaches to the human past and present.'[55] She continues:

> Martin thus comes to appreciate Honor's point of view by slow and patient constructive effort; in this respect *A Severed Head* is itself a love letter, written to and for Honor as well as about her, in all probability in answer to her searching, blinding questions. In attempting to explain to her actions inexplicable to himself and sometimes inexcusable by normal standards, Martin casts his story in an idiom hardly to be expected from a military historian, the language of myth he has learned from her.[56]

This view offers up an interesting possibility, although it demands much assuming that, perhaps, Murdoch does not wish to allow the reader. And, surely, such consciousings as I am now considering are a fugitive affair indeed. But the ambiguity in which the reader finds herself involved is a phenomenon to which she must continually and creatively respond. I think that *A Severed Head* is a species of literary work 'whose "basic and peculiar charm" ', as Robert Magliola would have it, resides 'precisely in the ambiguities contained. These ambiguities are "calculated for the full enjoyment of the esthetic characters based on 'irridescence' and 'opalescence'". Such literary works would lose their charm if one were to improve them by removing ambiguity.'[57] The 'spot of indeterminacy' to which the reader is responding at this level of engagement by 'supplying the missing links' and 'filling in the gaps' to resolve the ambiguity brings to the foreground the virtual dimension of the literary work which remained hidden or unrecognised during the first level of reading I have presented.

A different dimension of meaning is experienced if it is suspected in this story that Martin has, credibly enough, learned something that the reader is still struggling to learn. Thus, a deeper level of reading occurrs when we achieve an attitude of dwelling in the subsidiaries of Martin's consciousness. Approching the text in this way, we find that Martin has gained a dialectical awareness which might well be characterised, following Richard Palmer, as *hermeneutical* experience. To experience such an encounter is to engage in a structure of 'creative negativity', an experience that I would call creative misreading, brought to the reader's consciousness aptly by the dynamics of implicative irony in *A Severed Head*. Palmer writes:

> For to experience is to understand not better but differently; experience does not tell one what he expected, but tends to transcend and negate expectations. A 'deep' experience teaches us not to understand better what is already partially understood so much as that we were understanding wrongly.[58]

The point is that the ironic structure of Murdoch's text brings the reader up short, shatters his or her expectations, to unveil (Heidegger) or disclose (Ricoeur) a deeper awareness which derives from the text's world (as intended by a changed Martin) turning inside out and, as it were, inquiring of the reader, asking the reader the question of *his* or *her* horizon, demanding that the reader's somewhat fixed sensibility submit to expansion, to an openness not felt before the act of reading began.

But there is a way of going beyond this fixed horizon, for experience is a means of 'creative transcendence' which is admittedly moral in emphasis.[59] When any work of Murdoch's is encountered, the reader's understanding is challenged and perhaps transformed, for Murdoch would have our habitual way of seeing broken down, shaped anew. Murdoch holds that such a dialectical way of seeing will allow the text to interrogate the horizon of the reader, so that the experience of reading will comport with the fusion of the reader's and the text's horizons, by way of which 'a more encompassing understanding'[60] may emerge.

Surely it is known, as James Gindin put it more than two and a half decades ago, that 'man's 'interest in structure is, in Miss Murdoch's novels, part of his interest in precision, in defining himself and his world. Almost all of the characters in the novels seek some form of definition, some means of coherently explaining what they are'.[61] Dipple richly expands this secularly tempered theme of the quest for the good, for breakthroughs to reality:

> The distance between the character (finally *any* character, no matter how minor, since they are all totally absorbed in their particu-

larized quests, all *en route*) and the end he or she longs for is enormous and always in danger of becoming an uncrossable void. The subject of Murdoch's fiction is the methods devised by various kinds of consciousnesses to traverse that distance. The novels describe the cunning of the human mind in gathering useful tools for the crossing, and illustrate how the distance alters as the end invariably recedes and demands redefinition. Those who find the best answers and surest route (the few characters of good) decline to define the end at all; they concentrate on the route itself, the humble details of the means whereby we advance to the unimaginable.[62]

Now one cannot interpolate too much about the degree to which Martin has arrived at a personal answer to his 'nightmare'. The degree of irony might be clarified by further pursuing Murdoch's intentions in writing fiction. The novel before us bodies forth no clear resolution, and one can assume that Murdoch has intended this. The answer to whether or not Martin has such intentions resides in the power of the novel's suggestively ironic ambiguity. I have suggested that Murdoch is aware of this – certainly through the double persona of Bradley Pearson and his telling. And she has offered more information elsewhere – information including the first-person narrator's awareness of time (namely, time elapsed since events presented), the narrator's awareness of artistic style, and so on – perhaps most cleverly and compellingly in her justly praised work *The Sea, The Sea*.[63]

I have suggested that *A Severed Head* is significant because it can shape the response of its readers through what I have termed its hermeneutic strategy of implicative irony. I have argued for this perspective because I wish my criticism to be open to the reader's actual experience of this literary work, and to be responsive to the manifold complexities attending such experience. I have urged that, 'in elucidating how the facts might have been otherwise', a second reading of this text functions in such a way as to 'compel us to imagine the innerness and otherness of different ways of being, thinking, and feeling than our own'. [64]

I have shown that Murdoch is acutely aware of the effect particular bits of information will have on a careful rereader's formulation of meaning.[65] There is, I believe, a limit to all this: a writer (Murdoch) creates a character (Martin), who 'appears' (for the reader entangled within the implicatively ironic level of reading) to be as aware of the craft of narrative as Murdoch herself. Of course, if this were so, it would be the final awareness to which Martin might have arrived, at some point after the events described in his autobiographical account and before his writing of it. But this would take an extreme ironic leap indeed, one which *A Severed Head* does not, with such literal explicitness, support.

Rather, I conclude that the book suggests an intended ambiguity that cannot, finally, be resolved. I think that Martin might have arrived at the same conclusion. If the reader responds in the way I have suggested may be possible, she would be offered the possibility of experiencing and thinking otherwise because of such ironic implication. The form of otherness mediated to us by Martin is this experience he himself has intended, because (whether satisfied or not) he has learned to accept the reality of truth revealed through myth, conceiving of myth 'as, in the broad sense, hermeneutic. Its function is less to explain than to interpret, less to analyze or merely assert than to repossess and continue, ... ideally involv[ing] the whole person and not just the mind'.[66] Martin's awareness is a knowledge that the reader cannot (and ought not, if one follows Richard Palmer's argument) finally reduce to an explanation. Rather, one finds that it is too private, too opaque, too 'other', as Martin has been told by Honor, and as the reader, through Martin's implicatively ironic telling, has been told by Murdoch.

6

Conclusion: Religion, Literature and the Ethics of Reading Narrative

> Good reading is also productive, performative. Naming the text rightly, it brings the strange phosphorous of the life,... 'the radiant gist', back once more above ground.[1]
>
> The true novelist will restore the reality of the Other in all its actuality and visibility – its im-mediacy.[2]

I trust that the interpretative net I have flung over the preceding discussions has enabled us to see new connections, novel configurations between the text and reader, literature and religion, critical theory and the possible projects of the humanities. I use the word 'trust' because there is a very great mischief loosed upon us, one might imagine some in the field declaring deliberately, a very great noise indeed bruited throughout the precincts of religion and literature. The search for a basis of limitation for interpretation (Foucault), the sense of error in *any* grounding of meaning (Miller), the Barthian assurance of a surplus of signification, the argument advanced by Frank Kermode for the secrecy of a text as its available reserve, its potential for interpretation, the *Critical Inquiry* tanglings for and against interpretation – all these moves evidence an unnerving range of possible conflicting interpretations, and the *way* Melville, Joyce and Murdoch write may not lessen the options brought to bear on such discussions. If Chapter 2 has served as the theoretical armature of this study, spinning the skein through which the explicit chapters on the reading of narrative texts are offered, this conclusion is meant to be an act of reception of the foregoing discussions, yielding what for the reader might connect the field of religion and literature and reader-response criticism.

My book has selected narratives whose power sends us widdershins our readerly expectations. Though we may circumspectly read for the ending, the stories seem to resist closure, and our efforts to actualise their fascinating ambiguities point to their textual *frisson* as ethical armature from work to reader. Many narratives function just so in the way they communicate meaning (a fact not lost on Wayne Booth[3] – by page 6 of his book we find him stating with his characteristic comprehensiveness, 'no one seems to resist ethical criticism for long'), and I wish in the following brief discussion to suggest why such 'just so' stories have necessary ethical bearing on our understanding of religion and literature. It seems to me that presently it is the 'reader' who may help us in 'the discovery of where things are in relation to each other', to recall a phrase of Margaret Atwood.[4] Both Wolfgang Iser and Hillis Miller would agree but, to put it in the vernacular, they would agree differently. I want to focus on this difference, and to do so I wish first to go back to a point on the compass that helped us see the map we once knew, a mark known as 'Abrams', which was addressed in Chapter 2.

For about three decades, M. H. Abrams's model of the literary text and its historically realised relations with the world, the author and/or the audience has been acknowledged, revised and rarely rejected as a fruitful beginning for American understandings of those linkings betwixt and between religion and literature that allow for its promise as a significant interdiscipline. And although Abrams's position has been more recently bruited by Hillis Miller's animadversions, the model served as the organising paradigm for Giles Gunn's discussion of the various ways we might assess the connections between religious and literary concerns which have been advanced from antiquity. It was from this same model that, in a more recent discussion, Gunn detailed more fully a method of 'principled eclecticism'.[5] What Gunn has been led to assert 'beyond' this model is what I believe the model lacks, and this recognition very much brings into relief both certain developments in literary theory and my own portion of engagement in the field of religion and literature. As is now evident from the foregoing chapters, to my mind the historical and newer interests of the field can be enriched meaningfully when they are rendered and augmented in light of the insights being voiced by reader-response criticism.

Broadly speaking, religion and literature has been for some while experiencing a 'different turn'. Many in the field are now interested in the discussion of the relations of these two 'modes of awareness and expression' when they are brought, as Gunn would have it, to the plane of 'the hermeneutical,... the anthropological,... and the broadly humanistic'.[6] We recall that the discussion of Victor Turner,

Conclusion

for example, may be found informing the introductory chapter of Nathan Scott's book of 1985, *The Poetics of Belief*, and a few years ago Professor David Hesla remarked on the increased relevance of anthropology for considerations traditionally thought to be housed fully within the scape of theology and literature. For my purposes, the witness to the hermeneutical and anthropological in the field can bring us to that region which Wolfgang Iser has suggested might be denoted the 'anthropological side of literary criticism'.[7] My view is that we do not encounter a literary text as spectators but as readers seeking or discovering meaning(s) in the relations perceived and integrated into consciousness. As engaged readers, we may be seduced by the otherness of the literary work, ambushed by our unspoken expectations, or frustrated by the 'unwelcome cipher'[8] of the text before us. My chosen authors have a beguiling awarness of this, and indeed *will* this, and I have suggested possible ways in which certain of their tellers might now know this, too.

And it seems to me that we might therefore descry an increased acknowledgement in the ethical proportion accorded one's fuller account of the literary transaction with religion and narrative sensibility. Robert Detweiler, in his introductory editorial observations for the collection of essays, *Life on the Borders*,[9] sees such an ethical dimension to be both a curious lacuna in religion and literature studies and also one slowly yet steadily being brought back into current discussion. Indeed, an ally of such studies in years past, J. Hillis Miller, is currently engaged in advancing further his own route through the labyrinth of 'the order of words' in his writing of two books on *The Ethics of Reading*.[10]

Thus, in setting about the business of engaging questions of narrative in such modern literary works as *Moby-Dick*, *Ulysses*, *The Black Prince*, *A Severed Head* (or the many other texts we could find before us), narratives disruptive of the reader's expectations, we have found a host of insights drawn from reader-response criticism, hermeneutics and the 'turn to otherwise' in religion and literature to be both necessary and illuminating.

We have been led to note the distinctive kinds of pressure on the reader of such narratives in his or her appropriation of the text's otherness, and the metaphysical, epiphanic and hermeneutical forms of meaning that are experienced in the process of such reading. The foregoing chapters have attempted to limn the social ties of the shuttle, that dynamic noted above which Geoffrey Hartman finds as 'epiphanous resonance', Fredric Jameson as 'diachronic agitation', Wallace Stevens as 'a luminous flittering' flying back and forth through interpretative conventions between the reader and the text whereby meaning is encountered, recovered or engendered.

We have seen that this approach is concerned both with possible meanings of narratives and with the processes the reader engages in order to experience their significance. In the particular texts engaged above, narrative entanglement has led the reader often into ambiguity and away from the valorised need 'to anchor the work'[11] unimpeachably, to ground the literary meaning, say, in authorial intention, or in the world itself, because of 'the stubborn belief that the phenomenality of words somehow naturally corresponds to the essence of things'.[12] Such narratives as these impel the reader into a participative role, because each of these texts offers ironic forms of resistance, while yet proffering all the traditional enjoyments of a 'good story told'. I am reminded in this last instance of the remark made by Faulkner's daughter when he was reading *Moby-Dick* to her: 'Please read on; I want to find out what happens to thet whale.'

I have shown why acknowledgement of the reader's response is *fundamental* to our understanding of these works, of the experience of liminality that emerges through the actual experience of reading and, metaphysically, of the sense that 'the aboriginal reality is not the isolate self but a prior otherness with which the self must reckon'.[13] Hillis Miller has been at great pains recently to remind us all that 'reading is hard work' indeed, and that we are all, as participants in this postmodern world, under the 'obligation to read, carefully, patiently, with nothing taken for granted beforehand',[14] *not even* the 'warm life-world' behind or antecedent to language. (Miller faults Paul Ricoeur for just this position, the belief 'that there *is* an "outside-the-text" to which language refers'.[15])

From first to last, the final privileging of the hermeneutical over the formal has been a strategy taken by the field of religion and literature in order to move beyond formalism to the artist's (often existentialist, Scott and Hopper have remarked) vision; for me, it has encouraged the recognition of the importance of the experience of reading, of the reader's participation in what Keats once called 'richer entanglements'. I have said that this approach calls for the critic to dwell less on the text's origins and more on its tropical repetitions and effects. Accordingly, I have argued that the reader is necessarily constitutive of the overall actualised literary event.

Rather than calling for a 'sea-change' in our discussion of what might be religion and literature's necessary province, I am urging that we attempt a tacking into the linkings as they are *experienced* by us *as readers*, and that our tellings of homecoming from such voyaged slantings might modify how we go about the business of quickening, 'cure'-ing the interdiscipline. Wolfgang Iser and his focus on the reader's interpretative entanglement with the text provides a different understanding of the literary work from those offered by preceding grammars of the imagination generated or highlighted by the model of the literary work offered by Abrams and used by Lionel Trilling. Indeed, to move from Abrams's ordering to Wolfgang Iser's anthropology of literary criticism is to shift from an emphasis on a typology of possible readings to an attention directed to the active nature of the reading process itself. The interdiscipline of religion and literature can be enriched meaningfully, I firmly believe, by allowing its methods of interpretation to be informed by this perspective, especially as they presently bear on deepening our understanding of 'literature's formation of cultural reality'.[16] Indeed, in some measure such an appropriation has begun to occur. We find it in the fascination that Clifford Geertz and Kenneth Burke hold for Giles Gunn, that Victor Turner holds for Nathan Scott, and the overwhelming impact that Heidegger's phenomenology, first fully expressed by Stanley Romaine Hopper, holds continuously for the field in general as it pursues those links between a response to the sacred and the received traditions of the poetic imagination. Iser's work can help us to understand better 'human being' as it is understood in religious circles in terms of a threshold of the liminal. Iser observes:

> The interplay between the fictional and the imaginary provides the necessary heuristics for such an exploration. Fictionality in its boundary-crossing capacity, is first and foremost an extension of man which, like all operations of consciousness, is nothing but a pointer towards something other than itself.[17]

It is encouraging to find recent works which focus on the act of reading the great modern writers furthering such understanding: Robin Feurer Miller's *Dostoevsky and 'The Idiot'*,[18] Brook Thomas's *James Joyce's 'Ulysses'*,[19] Bainard Cowan's *Exiled Waters* and Warwick Wadlington's *Reading Faulknerian Tragedy* are splendid recent examples, and this book is indebted to them for helping me to understand and thereby articulate the reader's 'daunting entanglement with otherness'.[20]

II

> The text itself becomes a kind of junction where other texts, norms, and values meet and work upon each other; as a point of intersection its core is virtual, and only when actualized – by the potential recipient – does it explode into its plurivocity.[21]

As with many other approaches that have implicated extra-literary resources for the *necessary* understanding of the nature of narrative, we have seen especially in our discussion of Murdoch that Iser, too, adopts an extrinsic approach, though his preservation of an independent text existing prior to the act of reading signals a link with New Criticism that ought not be forgotten (nor *could* it be, Martin Price would add, for we continue to be 'haunted' by its hegemony[22]). The range of possible readings is broadened, it is true, but Iser still finds it meaningful to speak of limits to critical pluralism: the act of reading does recognise textual constraints. The most recent effort to wrestle with the ethical impact of such constraints is Wayne Booth's *The Company We Keep: An Ethics of Fiction*, and before I turn to Northrop Frye, a few remarks on Booth's work would be instructive.

Like Giles Gunn, Booth allows that each narrative, when brought to the mind of the reader, 'provides an alternative story set in a created "world" that is itself a fresh alternative to the "world" or "worlds" previously serving as boundaries of the reader's imagination.... [I]t determines to some degree *how at least this one moment will be lived'*. Booth claims the full measure of universality for his ethics of criticism (as does Frye), since the ethical effects of engaging with narratives are experienced by everyone. He writes: 'No human being, literate or not, escapes the effects of stories, because everyone tells them and listens to them.'[23] Now, from this full measure of universality of our experience of narrative, Booth notes that the ethics of narrative is a peculiarly *reflexive* study. None of us has lived a lifetime without narrative. None of us is an untouched soul (indeed, Booth appeals to Augustine's formulation, you must 'first believe in order to understand'). And the experience is *reciprocal*, for the teller is just as affected as the listener. Lastly, such ethical debate about narrative can lead almost instantaneously into ultimate questions.

Booth chastens Gabriel Josipovici's strategy of evaluative criticism, his declared expression, say, that Muriel Spark's supreme virtue is her ability to raise and sustain subtle questions about religious views of life. Josipovici reverences that possibility found in narrative when it is found to convey 'the continued tiny triumphs of questions over answers', rather than when, in most cases, it is 'on the side of those who know, of the masters of language and argument, on the side, that is, of God and the comforters'. Rather than reduce all narrative art to one universal standard, Booth proposes that we think of 'a botanical garden full of many beautiful species, each species implicitly bearing standards of excellence within its kind'.[24] After portraying several kinds of blanket attacks on this or that form of criticism, Booth several pages later returns to Josipovici for his conclusion:

> Of all the fashionable over-generalizations about ethical effect perhaps the most fashionable today is the one we have already encountered in Josipovici: the distinguishing virtue of literature is its power to lead us to questions rather than to answers; or, to 'open' the reader to new experiences of 'otherness'; or, to wake up the sleepy and complacent by disrupting previous fixities.[25]

Booth's responses to this favouring of a 'Universal Openness' are instructive, show why we could link Iser more on the side of Booth than otherwise, and allow for the recognition of the company we keep. He begins by insisting that there is no such thing as a *totally open work* – or, more accurately, even if there were, the reader of necessity would bring some closure to the text, 'in order to make *something* of it'.[26] And then Booth puts forward the observation that many had anticipated back in the late 1970s, a tenet most particularly brought into discussion by Iser:

> All successful narratives are constructed not of ideal total indeterminacy or total resolutions but of *limited determinacies* that by their vividness created strong suspensions or... 'instabilities': strong desires to continue in the company of *this* text to discover what kinds of openess or closure lie ahead.[27]

At its most profound, such openness 'serves a value that perhaps we all could embrace: genuine encounters with otherness, brought on by our invitation to grow by way of our ability to "internalize other selves" '.[28] And Booth then suggests that we arrive at our sense of the value of narratives in quite the same way that 'we arrive at the sense of value in persons: by *experiencing* them in an immeasurably rich context of others that are both like and unlike them.'[29]

Narratives have, in Booth's view, potential energy and thus are not 'predetermined to a single fulfillment'.[30] And it is here, within the precincts of a text's *virtuality*, that Booth is compelled to keep company with Iser most explicitly. A narrative experienced as *totally other* would of necessity be uninteresting – we would have no way of grasping its presentation. Contrariwise, a narrative totally familiar would be uninteresting to the point of boredom. Booth therefore rightly holds that 'the real distinctions of quality are found in kinds of otherness and kinds of familiarity. They are found finally not in how strange or "defamiliarized" the surface or "content" is but rather in what the reader is likely to learn about *ways of dealing with* the unfamiliar or the threatening'.[31]

There must be recognised the narrative realm between the totally other and the completely familiar that actively engages our imagination and relates our story to the larger story of humanity. As Wesley Kort notes:

> The relation of narrative art to experience, then, is the relation of articulated images to implied and often unconscious beliefs. Narrative art, by virtue of its form, matches the belief structure implied by an ongoing life. The beliefs...that can be inferred from a particular narrative may either reinforce or challenge the beliefs of its readers or hearers, but the potential for significant engagement between the beliefs of the narrative determined by its form and the belief structure of the reader is crucial to the relation of narrative to human life.[32]

Other notable ways of responding to the literary universe – say, Northrop Frye's – lead us to larger structures of the imagination that transcend, in some significant measure, the parameters of the 'objective theory' of the work of art appropriately characterised in American scholarship as New Criticism. I wish in the following section to present what, in my estimation, has been the most influential expression of such literary transcendence, the view put forward by Northrop Frye for two generations of literary and religious scholarship. I shall then turn, in the concluding section, to a final discussion of Iser.

III

> And this is where Frye's insistence on archetypes as the organizing principles of all imaginative activity, culminating in the *Anatomy of Criticism*, has a clarifying and disburdening effect. Blake himself claimed that his poetry was visionary rather than allegorical; it is indeed the *immediacy* of that mediated form called allegory which Blake tries to capture.... Frye recovers through Blake that naturally poetic language of the giants, and formulates it as a universal poetics, a grammar of archetypes.[33]

> These pregeneric mythoi, these models of all models, these deepest of structures which are the inevitable constituents of a literary imagination...are the fundamental object of the critical consciousness whose task is to receive those structures and communicate them to others.[34]

This section presents a discussion of one of the most provocative moments in modern literary critical history, Northrop Frye's *Anatomy of Criticism*.[35] For me, this remarkable text represents a suggestive application of the insights of Abrams's model of the literary work, an attention to the importance of symbol, and a brilliant consummation to the reach and relevance of archetypal criticism. Because this discussion of Frye follows our earlier discussion of Jung in Chapter 2, we will be reminded of various conceptual parallels between the two figures, even though Frye explicitly says that his concepts are not dependent on Jung's work. Our discussion of Coleridge may be recalled, too; if one assents to Robert Langbaum's judgement,[36] one can see that Frye is completing the thought of Coleridge. But broadly, Frye's is a celebration of the power of language, the lure of the 'order of words' felt by the imagination, and the place and practice of criticism in contemporary affairs of culture. I shall focus on key concepts found in the

'Polemical Introduction' and the 'Second Essay: Theory of Symbols' of *Anatomy of Criticism*.

From the outset of his book, Northrop Frye's synoptic vision of various extant procedures in literary criticism asks for nothing more than a fleshing out, or completion, of that which Aristotle intended by 'poetics'. This judgement, nevertheless, is not to deny Frye's own elevating, puzzling and richly suggestive contribution to the modern understanding of literary criticism. Indeed, his singular mythography may be viewed as striking or peculiar for at least three reasons. First, the very *intent* of Frye's scientific systematisation of critical procedures may disturb those who wish the practice of criticism to be safely removed from the arena of science and placed, perhaps, more closely to the art form with which it deals. Secondly, Frye employs various (and sometimes changing) definitions for words often understood more commonly to mean something else (for example, his definitions of 'symbol', 'ethical' and 'formalism'). Thirdly, Frye's idealistic hopes raise to the surface unchallenged principles that, one may finally estimate, actually *do* elude and mystify. This is perhaps most evident in the discussion of the anagogic phase of symbolism, wherein pure literary possibility may seem entirely detached from the realm of reality.

However idiosyncratic the book may be in one's final assessment, the scope of Frye's endeavour, initially expressed in the 'Polemical Introduction', is indeed both vast and synoptic. The gesture of embracing multiple facets of critical phenomena recognises, for example, both the point of view of the work of art itself (hence, the hypothesis of a 'still center of the order of words'), and that of the reader's encounter, the latter of which insists, cumulatively, on a heuristic pull 'toward a center of imaginative experience' (*AC*, 117).

Thus, Frye is flexible enough to include inductively both the suggestiveness of a single work of art and the numerous attitudes of practising approaches of criticism. This ranges from the 'profound masterpiece' which 'draws us to a point at which we seem to see an enormous number of converging patterns of significance' (*AC*, 17), to the hope that if only 'varied interests of critics could be related to a central expanding pattern of systematic comprehension' (*AC*, 12), sense and direction 'toward making the whole of literature intelligible' (*AC*, 9), and truer realisation of liberal education would soon follow. Culturally speaking, such an 'ethical' criticism 'should show a steady advance toward undiscriminating catholicity' (*AC*, 25).

Insisting on the necessity of a plurality of meanings ('polysemous meaning') within a work of literature, which consequently leads to the present variety of criticisms, Frye is concerned that we avoid the sterile, hackneyed situation of a pure relativity of value-judgements. In fact, he is on this point so sensitive to the proclamations of any comparative hierarchical standard of values that he wants criticism to focus only on what may be critically enlightening ('positive') about a poem. Anything else may be catalogued as merely another item in the history of taste. More primary, in Frye's design, is his expressed hope that 'it should be possible to get a comprehensive view of what literary criticism is actually doing' (*AC*, 12).

An interpenetating matrix of verbal associations, when universally expanded, is called by Frye the 'order of words'. Because this concept is quite central to the discussion which follows, it would be well to emphasise it at this time. It must be remembered that this poetic universe owes ultimate allegiance only to itself, and is independent of the systems of history (action) and philosophy (thought), regardless, historically, of what past experience in critical practice has adopted. I mean to suggest that this independence is qualified, for the poetic universe surely uses history and philosophy mimetically; the point is that it cannot be subsumed under either system.

Frye's systematisation of the ways in which symbols operate, as understood by corresponding modes of perception, does not suggest an infinite number of either critical approaches or symbolic modes. Frye seems to feel that only a finite number of 'phases' can lead to a firm possibility of defining an order of words which literary criticism, in its broadest prospect, could locate. The phases, then, which portray these different ways in which narrative and meaning relate to a symbolic context, often appear roughly to parallel major critical schools already familiar to the student of modern literature. Furthermore, these phases, with one addition, are, as Frye reminds us, merely modifications of the four phases distinguished in mediaeval literary criticism.

Although I have already employed the term 'phase', Frye variously denotes the different symbolic modes of units of literary structure as 'levels', 'phases' and 'types'. He most often uses the second term, perhaps because it lends itself to the suggestion of a *way* of seeing a symbol function. Just as importantly, it offers the sense of the possibility of a *sequence* of ('polysemous') meanings while avoiding the hierarchical advance of value connoted by the term 'level', of the notion of static fixation connoted by the term 'type'.

Frye descries five phases of literary symbolism, many of which ought to recall the application of Abrams's model grounding much of this chapter: the literal, the descriptive, the formal, the mythical and the anagogic. Because he defines 'symbol' as 'any unit of any literary structure that can be isolated for critical attention' (*AC*, 71), each phase focuses on a distinctive choice of symbol: motif, sign, image, archetype and monad.

Basic to any reader's experience is the polarity of attention that is directed inward, within the literary work itself, centripetally, literally, and outward, to the natural world, centrifugally, descriptively:

> In both cases we deal with symbols, but when we attach an external meaning to a word we have, in addition to the verbal symbol, the thing represented or symbolized by it.... Symbols so understood may... be called *signs*, verbal units which, conventionally and arbitrarily, stand for and point to the things outside the place where they occur. (*AC*, 73)

> Verbal elements understood inwardly or centripetally, as parts of a verbal structure, are, as symbols, simply and literally verbal elements, or units of verbal structure. We may... call such elements *motifs*. (*AC*, 73–4)

Now, if these types of structures are classified by the criterion of the ultimate direction of meaning, as Frye thinks they can be, then one notes that descriptive and assertive writing is radically distinguished from all literary verbal structures. The final direction of meaning for the former is outward, that of the latter, as evidenced in the historical movement of *symbolisme*, and refined in the more recent attention of the New Critics, is inward. New Criticism, that is, treats the poem as 'literally' a poem, and inspects its involuting ironies, metaphors and ambiguities in terms of that procribed assertion. Any purchase of meaning prehended from without necessarily creates a centrifugal movement within the work of art, for those items brought up for inspection will be placed, finally, in the province of the critic's assertive framework doing the inspecting.

Frye, of course, does not let the matter of meaning rest here; if he did, there would be no reach 'beyond formalism' to disturb and excite critical interest for decades. When one views the symbol as functioning as an image, one has entered the formal phase, and its consequent critical methodology, which instances the procedure, in W. K. Wimsatt's term, of explicitation – a practice which, as shall be seen, distinguishes it from the New Criticism:

> Formal criticism begins with an examination of the imagery of a poem, with a view to bringing out its distinctive pattern. The recurring or most frequently repeated images form its tonality, so to speak, and the modulating, episodic, and isolated images relate themselves to this in a hierarchic structure which is the critical analogy to the proportions of the poem itself. (AC, 85)

> The analysis of recurrent imagery is, of course, one of the chief techniques of rhetorical or 'new' criticism, after attaching the imagery to the central form of the poem renders an aspect of form into the propositions of discursive writing. Formal criticism, in other words, is commentary, and commentary is the process of translating into explicit or discursive language what is implicit in the poem. (AC, 86)

Now this 'process of translating', of commentary, is manifestly an allegorical act of interpretation, for it appends (culturally interesting) ideas to that which is the imagery in the poetic structure. Those symbols which are images of things are lifted from the poem by the critic but, because they can only be critically expressed propositionally, arrive for the reader in the rendered form of abstractions. This is the context suggested by my statement near the end of the discussion of Jung: criticism is not actually part of the work of art, and does not connect with its essence where 'genuine mystery' and the 'real place for wonder' (AC, 88) reside. As noted earlier, when the reader engages the mythical phase, symbols are seen to function as archetypes.

Archetypes, variably complex, are thought by Frye to be essentially units of communication, extending associations from a particular poem to poetry, on the one hand, and to a given culture, on the other. In this 'penultimate phase'[37] one is two steps away from pure *symbolisme*, and one is now viewing an aspect of symbols which the New Critics thought either unnecessary or critically unwarranted. The archetypal critic may view the phenomenon of poetry 'as part of the total human imitation of nature that we call civilization' (*AC*, 104–5).

Thus, the notion of the externally relational aspect of poetry – that of viewing a poem not in isolation and as an imitation of nature but as a unit of poetry, as participating in an imitation of other poems – now brings criticism to a new task: the necessity of discerning that aspect of symbolism which relates one poem to another, and that relates one poem to an order of words.

As mentioned earlier, the reader at this point approaches a vital tenet of Frye's theory of criticism, namely, this positing of 'an order of words' which, correspondingly, imitates the order of nature. Any time a reader engages imaginatively with a work of literature, he or she unconsciously relates it to other works. Every work is a manifestation, or a realised form, if you will, of the 'order of words', of, as Frye once called it, 'the universal spirit of poetry' (*AC*, 98).

The structure of poetry provides the forms into which the content of the world is poured. A symbolic transformation is brought about, the content of which is no less communicable than discursive verbal units of meaning. It is upon this communicable – this *social* – aspect of poetry that the archetypal critic focuses his or her attention. The archetype is the symbol of the communicable unit. It is, then, for Frye

> a typical or recurring image. I mean by an archetype a symbol which connects one poem with another and thereby helps to unify and integrate our literary experience. And as the (un-Jungian) archetype is the communicable symbol, archetypal criticism is primarily concerned with literature as a social fact and as a mode of communication. By the study of conventions and genres, it attempts to fit poems into the body of poetry as a whole. (*AC*, 99)

The energy that lures human society to give form to the experienced world is *desire*, the point of presence that, as Frank Lentricchia writes:

> is the deepest human center of governance; it is not the property of a single, differentiated subject, but the intersubjective force which impels all activity of expression, all civilizing humanization and ordering of an indifferent and stupid nature. By remaining free of all transformation, as a kind of secular *primum mobile*,

itself unmoved, desire is the sure ground, the guarantee of Frye's ultimate humanism.[38]

The element of *recurrence* in life is reflected in that narrative aspect of literature denoted *ritual*. The conflict between desire and reality provides the significance content of literature (this is suggested by the principle of *dream*). In the phase we are now considering, the poem imitates nature as a cyclical process, and the archetypal critic discerns those ritualistic expressions of natural recurrence such as the sun, the moon, the seasons and so forth. The interpretation of recurrence and desire provides for complex assignations to ritual and dream:

> Poetry in its social or archetypal aspect... not only tries to illustrate the fulfillment of desire, but to define the obstacles to it. Ritual is not only a recurrent act, but an act expressive of a dialectic of desire and repugnance: desire for fertililty or victory, repugnance to drought or to enemies.... In dream there is a parallel dialectic, as there is both the wish-fulfillment dream and the anxiety or nightmare dream of repugnance. Archetypal criticism, therefore, rests on two organizing rhythms or patterns, one cyclical, the other dialectic.
> The union of ritual and dream in a form of verbal communication is myth.... The myth accounts for, and makes communicable, the ritual and the dream. Ritual, by itself, cannot account for itself: it is pre-logical, pre-verbal, and in a sense pre-human. (*AC*, 106)

> Myth ... not only gives meaning to ritual and narrative to dream: it is the identification of ritual and dream, in which the former is seen to be the latter in movement.... [R]itual is the archetypal aspect of *mythos* and dream the archetypal aspect of *dianoia*. (*AC*, 107)

It is obvious that genetic hegemony could easily determine the necessary relationships among literary criticism, anthropology's interest in ritual and psychology's interest in dream. Frye is careful to say that the literary critic has no interest in the historical *origins* of ritual and dream (and this, I suppose, is why he makes such brief note of the influences of Sir James Frazer and Carl Jung). The archetypal critic, rather, focuses on the relationship of content to form, of ritual and dream patterns within the literary structure. The sources of such content are precluded by definition of the critic's proper place and practical task. (It is interesting to note that this same understanding of preclusion is held by such 'new' Jungian critics as James Hillman.)

Thus, under the aegis of archetypal symbols, art, as a part of civilisation, shares in the human formulations of the natural world. This is why such symbols are natural objects invested with human meaning. This view also encourages a distinction from the Platonic notion of 'recollection', of poetry as a penultimate imitation of reality. Frye interprets mimesis, rather, as a freeing of the objective world into the form of images, of nature into art (as does Paul Ricoeur). Art can finally be related only to, and within, itself. Literature is non-discursive, and by definition its verbal units of meaning do not function descriptively.

And yet, Frye argues that the archetypal phase cannot be the last, for within its mythic confinements, poetry cannot be dissociated from the civilisation of which it plays a part:

> The archetypal view of literature shows us literature as a total form and literary experience as a part of the continuum of life, in which one of the poet's functions is to visualize the goals of human work. As soon as we add this approach to the other three, literature becomes an ethical instrument, and we pass beyond Kierkegaard's 'Either/Or' dilemma between aesthetic idolatry and ethical freedom, without any temptation to dispose of the arts in the process. Hence the importance, after accepting the validity of this view of literature, of rejecting the external goals of morality, beauty, and truth. The fact that they are external makes them idolatrous, and so demonic. But if no social, moral, or aesthetic standard is in the long run externally determinative of the value of art, it follows that the archetypal phase, in which art is part of civilization, cannot be the ultimate one. We need still another phase where we can pass from civilization, where poetry is still useful and functional, to culture, where it is disinterested and liberal, and stands on its own feet.   (*AC*, 115)

As I suggested at the beginning of this section, it is this fifth, or anagogic, phase which is most 'elevating' and 'puzzling'. The mythopoeic scope has not been left behind, but narrowed, so that themes of the divine are discerned. Frye believes that the positing of archetypes necessitates, by that very supposition, conceiving the possibility of a self-contained order of words, a literary universe which embraces both the unlimited potential of life, and those particulars instanced in a single poem. In other words, one must assume a total form of literature. Because of this, one finds that the literature most resonant with the anagogic phase is scripture and apocalyptic revelation.

What the anagogic critic finds is a nexus of universal symbols located within the centre of archetypes. Frye calls a symbol of this kind a monad, for it posits the centre of the literary universe in any poem currently engaging the reader's mind, while concurrently promoting the conception of a poem as a microcosm of the order of words. Frye is noticeably spatial in the choice of metaphors regarding his idea of anagogy, as he has been in his conception of locating a 'centre', a 'still point', about which extant literary practices revolve. The anagogic phase involves not the actual, but the possible; it is a realm of 'inscape', of 'epiphany', of, in a word, the infinite. The terms employed in suggesting the archetypal – nature, ritual, dream, desire – are therein transformed:

> When we look at the dream as a whole, we notice three things about it. First, its limits are not the real, but the conceivable. Second, the limit of the conceivable is the world of fulfilled desire emancipated from all anxieties and frustrations. Third, the universe of the dream is entirely within the mind of the dreamer.
>
> In the anagogic phase, literature imitates the total dream of man, and so imitates the thought of a human mind which is at the circumference and not at the center of its reality... When we pass into anagogy, nature become, not the container, but the thing contained, and archetypal universal symbols... are no longer the desirable forms that man constructs inside nature, but are themselves the forms of nature. Nature is now inside the mind of an infinite man who builds his cities out of the Milky Way. This is not reality, but it is the conceivable or imaginative limit of desire, which is infinite, eternal, and hence apocalyptic. (*AC*, 119)

Apparently, the anagogic phase functions somewhat as an encyclopaedic gesture: poetry, within such vast compass, imitates ritual as unlimited social action, and dream as total, or unlimited, individual thought. It influences literary revelations of divinity expressed in human form. This phase is as close as is legitimately possible for criticism to be connected with religion.

It is within the anagogic phase that Frye conceives literature as harbouring a universal container of the possibilities of life, realised in the multifarious verbal relationships arranged in the form of monads. We have arrived at the highest level of imaginative experience.

Much of this, I think, is structured towards Frye's wish for literature and criticism to have a liberalising impact on culture. The critic's sensitivity for that in literature which transcends the bounds of civilisation's moral restrictions is to be applauded. One is not surprised, therefore, to discover such comments as the following: 'The study of literature takes us toward seeking poetry as the imitation of infinite social action and infinite human thought, the mind of a man who is all men, the universal creative word which is all words' (*AC*, 125); 'the study of literature belongs to the "humanities", and the humanities, as their name implies, can take only the human view of the superhuman' (*AC*, 126); 'it is of the essence of imaginative culture that it transcends the limits both of the naturally possible and of the morally acceptable' (*AC*, 127). Considering such remarks, it may be seen that Frye has set up a grand design for criticism, such that there may be a place – the symbol in its anagogic phase – wherein the 'human view of the superhuman' may be located.

In bringing this section to a close, I wish to emphasise the rigour with which Frye calls for an inductive experiencing of literature as the *sine qua non* of his critical universe. Although the tendency may be natural and necessarily practical, one will not get to the real backbone of Frye's criticism if one dwells solely in an argument about how particular examples match up with archetypes and myths and modes. As with most systematics in philosophy and theology, all the parts of the structured argument are, finally, going to fit – even if patterns become overlarge and clumsy, or simply incredible. Frye would admit, however, that if his overall schema is weak, one would find it so by an inductive engagement with literature *per se*. This approach paradoxically locates criticism within, but not part of, the 'order of words': 'The presence of incommunicable experience in the center of criticism will always keep criticism an art, as long as the critic recognizes that criticism comes out of it but cannot be built on it' (*AC*, 27–8). I now turn to a last discussion of Wolfgang Iser's significance for this study.

III

If it is true, as I am suggesting, that poetic patterns are not learned by the poet primarily through the study of other poet's works but are his own unthematized and spontaneous response to the same reality that mystified primitive man... one has to wonder about the universality of the fundamental mystery that gives rise to these patterns. 'The thing I hum appears to be/The rhythm of this celestial pantomime'. That mystery is threefold in its composition of man's relation to some transcendent 'other', and his relation with the 'other' that is discovered in himself. Presumably, if language is the creation that grapples with this mystery, then each language will develop certain figural strategies.[39]

Iser's work, as a theory of reader-oriented criticism, represents another shift away from New Criticism, especially away from its tenet, as Walter Benn Michaels expresses it, 'that *literary* language, at least, is "non-referential" (i.e., that it can be understood neither as the representation of an external and prior "reality")', or away from those New Critical strategies, that is to say, 'made necessary by the fear of subjectivity, of the individual interpreter's self.'[40] It is a shift, writes Jane Tompkins (in perhaps the finest historical overview of these issues), motivated particularly by the opposition to the 'belief that meaning inheres completely and exclusively in the literary text'.[41] I hasten to add that I think New Criticism continues to give us a rich platform for critical discussion, since it reminds us of the concept of literary autonomy and the hesitation of modern critical thought to make uniform claims about the relationship of literature to the objective world.

My intention is not at all to have my observations pass for literary history, but rather to observe certain kinds of readerly resistance which invite certain forms of coherence. Indeed, as Richard Poirier has recently remarked, 'The kinds of coherencies we should start looking for ought to have less to do with chronology or periods than with habits of reading.'[42]

I find two major tasks being accomplished by Iser's theory. He shows the obvious relevance of phenomenology to the experience of reading a literary text. Secondly, in recent years Iser has given noteworthy attention to the dynamic, contextual dimension of the literary event called 'virtuality'. It is his phenomenological discussion of the 'virtuality' of a text – the relation, that is, which necessarily transpires between the text and the reader during the act of reading – which I believe can help those of us in religion and literature to speak in novel ways about the experience of narrative 'meaning'.

And as should now be evident, it is this vital, 'virtual' dimension that Abrams neglects to account for in his model of the text and its relationships to the world, the audience, the author and itself. Iser is quite right to stress two dimensions of literature: the fact that literature must be viewed as an 'event' if it is to be experienced at all, and that it can only 'be' because of its virtuality. This paradox is evident in the dialectical paradigm provided by Iser. The reading referent is beheld as a literary object, and yet such objective referentiality can only be experienced as manifest through the reader's horizon of expectations, those readerly conventions that allow meaning to come into being by way of the act of reading. Literature must be understood 'relationally'.

Iser offers one of his clearest brief statements early in *The Act of Reading*: 'As the text and reader thus merge into a single situation, the division between subject and object no longer applies, and it therefore follows that meaning is no longer an object to be defined, but is an effect to be experienced.'[43] The point to be emphasised here is that the concretisation of a text in any particular instance requires that the reader's imagination come into play. But it must also be admitted that, in the last account, the text's intentions can be traceable to the work itself. In contrast to this view, Jonathan Culler, whose voice has sounded in much of this book, holds that literary meaning is not the result of a reader responding to an author's cues (the intentional 'gaps' valued by Iser) but is a social matter, a function of conventions that are publicly agreed upon. Culler's poetics of literary competence, that is, attends more to the 'tacit knowledge or competence which underlies'[44] the behaviour of reading, and less to the actual performance of a real reader reading.

A unifying aspect of the approach I would encourage is the common concern for *receiving* the otherness presented by the texts read. Iser is important here because he allows us to adopt a critical strategy pragmatically 'based on a theory of reading'.[45] The focus is as much on the reader as on the literary works, and this attention bears the contextual experience of virtuality. If one's practical criticism is in general agreement with Iser's position, it will accordingly reflect the contemporary shift in critical perspective described by

Susan Suleiman as a general movement 'away from the formalist and New Critical emphasis on the autonomy of "the text itself" toward a recognition (re-recognition) of the relevance of context, whether the latter be defined in terms of historical, cultural, ideological, or psychological categories'.[46] What one must avoid is the presumption that the meaning of a literary text is a given, an 'in-itself', which needs only to be unfolded, peeled back to a stable essence (recall the voiced concerns of Hillis Miller, above, or the postmodern suspicions of any sense of essentialisation, generally), because all acts of understanding, as Hans Robert Jauss shows in his work, are necessarily situated and received in an historical setting. From this vantage point, much in recent hermeneutical discussion makes immediate sense, especially when 'meaning' is no longer understood to be possessed by and in the semantically autonomous text itself. But rather than siding with E. D. Hirsch who holds that meaning depends finally upon authorial intention, I side with Iser in my concern for the intersubjective process of reading as an essential determinant of the meaning of the literary text. David Couzens Hoy's work, *The Critical Circle*, qualifies this view by stating:

> The meaning of the text is in *one* sense the meaning given by the interpreter, since the text poses a question to him in his particular historical situation and he approaches the text with given expectations. But in a larger sense it can be said that the projection is a function of the text itself, for the interpreter can test his expectations against the text. The meaning of the text can claim the interpreter only insofar as it comes from beyond him and transcends him.[47]

Giles Gunn carefully leans in this direction, too, although he qualifies his assertion: 'The critic's method is to saturate the text with meanings, meanings which, strictly speaking, the text does not contain solely within itself.'[48]

In contrast with Roman Ingarden's adherence to the concept of organic unity as the basic criterion for the reader's concretisation,[49] Iser establishes, as Rudolf Kuenzli rightly notes, 'indeterminacy as the basic condition for communication'. We have witnessed ways in which Iris Murdoch is marvelously adept in the uses she makes of this insight. Kuenzli continues, 'In defining the function of the literary work...as triggering the reader's imagination in order to recognize the limitations of his habitual norms and codes, Iser rejects the concept of organic unity as a criterion for adequate concretization, and he pragmatizes the aesthetic experience.'[50]

And so Iser's communication model of reading emphasises 'meaning-production', meaning experienced by the reader. But note that I have tried to show how the text of *Moby-Dick*, of *Ulysses* and of *A Severed Head* serves as limiter to the reader's assembling of meaning. In *Interpretive Conventions*, Steven Mailloux writes: 'Iser explicitly posits a preexistent text which interacts with the reader and in that interaction restricts the reader's interpretations.... Though Iser does assume a stable text of some kind, his rhetoric emphasizes the creative role of the reader.'[51] To continue the contrast between Culler and Iser, these 'limits' for Culler derive from the competence of the reader as she or he creates the structure of the text being read. He most often focuses on those moments when the reading exceeds the norms of the employed social reading model, on 'the violent engagement with the conventional novelistic expectations of readers and the disruption of their habitual processes of sense-making'.[52] The common ground linking Iser and Culler to the possibilities of the religion and literature interdiscipline is the favouring of 'norm-breaking texts', narratives which, in Iser's words, bring about 'the pressure of the unfamiliar',[53] and which, in our response as readers, encourage us, as Culler would have it, to accede to 'a process of discovery'.[54] (The uncommon ground is Culler's tremendous antipathy to religious sensibility, as explicitly expressed in *Framing the Sign*.[55])

Obviously, the organising symbolic mode around which much contemporary critical thought has gathered is the status of the literary text, and more particularly the vexing notion that meaning no longer is possessed by the text itself. It seems to me that the principle of the imagination has been reconstituted at this horizon, where text meets reader in such a way that the reader actively co-creates, in some significant measure, the nature of the meaning experienced, without suffering the impressionistic consequences of 'The Affective Fallacy' which rightly concerned William Wimsatt and Monroe Beardsley in the late 1940s. I am suggesting that this is where the religious significance of the work is to be found.

J. Hillis Miller's most important function at present might well be his unflinching reminder to all of us that theory can make our reading opaque to ourselves, that theory can master the reading experience so 'already' that the result is a winning resistance to reading.[56]

Conclusion 139

Iser surely is aware of this too, but, as I noted earlier, he tacitly continues to presuppose, as do I, much more about the value-filled world beyond the text than Miller is ever again willing to grant. Miller's quest is for the rhetorical trace in a narrative that shimmers behind or underneath the theme, that flickering 'quick now, here now' seen by T.S. Eliot that must needs be found as *fundamentally opening, inaugural*, and thus be experienced as 'a breaking down and breaking open of one's old way of seeing', as, in a word, 'disruptive'.[57]

I think the field of religion and literature has been potentially engaged in the perspective on experience voiced by reader-response criticism since the late 1960s, and this can be seen easily by its quick accomodation to the hermeneutic programme charted by Hans-Georg Gadamer. It was to the experience of the *instability* of the chosen works – what, indeed, Gadamer claims is characteristic of our interpretative encounter with any literary work – that the field felt encouraged to direct its energies, especially as they bore renewed attention to the narrative polyvocality of traditional sacred texts.

The liminal tellings of Melville, Joyce and Murdoch lure the reader into an attentive participation in the complex texture of narrative telling; this is what their texts place before us, and we *know* we cannot refuse this invitation of imaginative encounter with otherness lest we resist entirely the recalcitrant power of the text – which is, after all, one of the 'points' of the stories as they call us into dialogue. In each instance, I have argued, we are made mindful, through our response, in a new and poised way, of the ethical recovery of who we might become. Such mindful responsiveness is here, with such narratives, rendered in astonishingly vivid, unforgettable detail, as the narratives trace such mimetic recovery in and through the dynamic of narration itself: in and through the movement of time, in and through the redemptive or defamiliarising irridescence of the narrative tellings and, finally, out and through the generative imagination of the reader. In such wise does narrative offer such disclosure of reality, of the 'strange phosphorus of life', engaging us, in Murdoch's necessary phrase, by way of 'a sense of otherness'.

In taking further account of the reader's experience of a literary work, we have seen that there has been a dialectic unfolding in the foregoing chapters. We might think of this as a dialectic between a religious sense of otherness engaged as an ideal whole always felt behind a particular reading, and as a sense of otherness revealed by its 'difference' from such unity. That is, on the one hand, 'the truth we encounter in otherness is of a whole; it cannot be claimed or fabricated. It must be received and discerned'.[58] On the other, the reader has been invited to reckon with an alternative to much in the Western tradition that subsumes otherness in the name of this larger unity, to experience an alternative to a tradition of idealism whereby 'otherness...seems to be both saluted and domesticated within a larger, overarching totality'.[59]

Joanne Frye has recently written, in *Living Stories, Telling Lives*: 'Through participating in the narrative constructions of literary characters, readers become better prepared to develop new narrative constructions of their own experience.'[60] Such an observation is particularly helpful when a reader finds herself entangled in a text that disrupts her *conventional* expectations, those moments where the 'gaps' in a telling are noticed and function as indeterminacies which involve the reader in narrative participation. Each of my selected narratives functions as a story of 'asymmetry and counterpoise',[61] and they engage us already in 'the fundamental asymmetry between text and reader'[62] experienced as metaphysical, epiphanic or hermeneutic readings of otherness. They function as tellings with a difference, for they continually embrace and break down and then build up our narrative assumptions, keep us engaged by an uncanny disruption of our efforts to place the space of 'then', for then continues to open into the moment of reading, from life to 'that rock of otherness constituted at last by death our death',[63] or from death to life, or (as Northrop Frye would note) from memory to desire and ultimately, from outside the literary universe to within, not only as 'unfinished' tellings realised by named or nameless tellers, but also as tellings actualised by and for us. Although we may find ourselves, with Ishmael, left 'without rescue', yet, as readers, *implicated* by the 'ineluctibly interpretive aspect',[64] of these epiphanic encounters, we find ourselves turning from the book, from the text to 'the sudden spiritual manifestation' of the world beheld by these three authors. We are renewed, in Wallace Steven's words, as if by 'a power again – That gives a candid kind to everything.'[65] By all accounts, we are lured into liminal involvements by way of our imagination that affect our concord with ordinary life.

Notes

Notes to Chapter 1: Reader's Share in the Narrative Events

1. Geoffrey Hartman, *Beyond Formalism* (New Haven, Conn.: Yale University Press, 1970) p. x.
2. Justis George Lawler, *Celestial Pantomime: Poetic Structures of Transcendence* (New Haven, Conn.: Yale University Press, 1979) p. 41.
3. Mark Schorer, 'An Interpretation', in Ford Maddox Ford, *The Good Soldier* (New York: Vintage Books, 1951) p. v.
4. J. Hillis Miller, review of *The Interpretation of Otherness*, by Giles Gunn, in *Journal of Religion*, 62 (July 1982) p. 303.
5. Wayne Booth, for example, acknowledges this story dimension when he writes that 'in the beginning, and from then on, there was story, and it was largely in story that human beings were created and now continue to recreate themselves'. See Wayne Booth, *The Company We Keep: An Ethics of Fiction* (Berkeley, Cal.: University of California Press, 1988) p. 39.
6. Philip Wheelwright, *The Burning Fountain: A Study in the Language of Symbolism* (Bloomington, Ind.: Indiana University Press, 1954) p. 8.
7. Northrop Frye's theory of symbols in 'Ethical Criticism', the second chapter of *Anatomy of Criticism: Four Essays* (Princeton, N.J.: Princeton University Press, 1957), will remind us at this point of former understandings and possible revisions of religion and literature's relationship to the reader's world.
8. Booth, *The Company We Keep*, p. 32.
9. Edward Said, *Beginnings: Intention and Method* (Baltimore, Md: Johns Hopkins University Press, 1975) p. 9.
10. Peter L. Berger, *The Heretical Imperative: Contemporary Possibilities of Religious Affirmation* (Garden City, NY: Anchor Press/Doubleday, 1979) p. 161.
11. Fredric Jameson, *The Political Unconscious: Narrative as a Socially Symbolic Act* (Ithaca, NY: Cornell University Press, 1981) p. 142.
12. Vernon Ruland, S.J., *Horizons of Criticism: An Assessment of Religious–Literary Options* (Chicago, Ill.: American Library Association, 1975) p. 117.
13. Paul Brodtkorb, *Ishmael's White World: A Phenomenological Reading of 'Moby Dick'* (New Haven, Conn.: Yale University Press, 1965) p. 53.
14. Most critics through the middle decades of the present century, including Gunn, have focused more on Ahab's struggle than on Ishmael's 'plurality of being', his nature as storyteller.
15. Richard H. Brodhead, *Hawthorne, Melville and the Novel* (Chicago, Ill.: University of Chicago Press, 1976) p. 154.
16. William T. Noon, S.J., *Joyce and Aquinas* (New Haven, Conn.: Yale University Press, 1959) p. 74.

17. Jonathan Culler, *Structuralist Poetics: Structuralism, Linguistics, and the Study of Literature* (Ithaca, NY: Cornell University Press, 1976) p. 261.
18. Said, *Beginnings*, p. 43.
19. Culler, *Structuralist Poetics*, p. 158.
20. Nathan Scott, *The Poetics of Belief* (Chapel Hill, N.C.: University of North Carolina Press, 1985) p. 3.
21. Peter S. Hawkins, *The Language of Grace: Flannery O'Connor, Walker Percy, and Iris Murdoch* (Cambridge, Mass.: Cowley Publications, 1983) p. 117.
22. Giles Gunn, *The Culture of Criticism and the Criticism of Culture* (New York: Oxford University Press, 1987) p. 85.
23. J. Hillis Miller, *Fiction and Representation* (Cambridge, Mass.: Harvard University Press, 1982) pp. 19–20.
24. Ibid., p. 176.
25. John Coulson, 'Religion and Imagination (Relating Religion and Literature)', in David Jasper (ed.), *Images of Belief in Literature* (New York: St Martin's Press, 1984) p. 19.

Notes to Chapter 2: Limning the Literary Universe

1. George Steiner, *Real Presences* (London: Faber & Faber, 1989) p. 206.
2. Iris Murdoch, 'Against Dryness: a Polemical Sketch', *Encounter*, 16 (January 1961) p. 20.
3. Inge Crosman Wimmers, *Poetics of Reading: Approaches to the Novel* (Princeton, N.J.: Princeton University Press, 1988) p. 21.
4. Albert Gelpi, *A Coherent Splendor: The American Poetic Renaissance, 1910–1950* (Cambridge: Cambridge University Press, 1987) p. 7.
5. Giles Gunn, *The Culture of Criticism and the Criticism of Culture* (New York: Oxford University Press, 1987) p. 181.
6. S. Bruce Kaufman, 'Charting a Sea-Change: On the Relationships of Religion and Literature to Theology', *Journal of Religion*, 58 (1978) p. 422.
7. Ibid., p. 424.
8. Giles Gunn, *The Interpretation of Otherness: Literature, Religion and the American Imagination* (New York: Oxford University Press, 1979) pp. 76–7.
9. Wesley Kort, *Narrative Elements and Religious Meaning* (Philadelphia, Pa: Fortress Press, 1975) p. 11.
10. David Jasper, *The Study of Literature and Religion* (London: Macmillan, 1989).
11. Plato, *The Dialogues of Plato*, trans. Benjamin Jowett, quoted in Hazard Adams (ed.), *Critical Theory since Plato* (New York: Harcourt, Brace, Jovanovich, 1971) p. 35.
12. Aristotle, *Poetics*, ch. xxv. in ibid., p. 64.
13. Gerald Graff, *Literature against Itself: Literary Ideas in Modern Society* (Chicago, Ill.: University of Chicago Press, 1979) p. 11.
14. Ernst Cassirer, *The Philosophy of Symbolic Forms*, trans. Ralph Manheim (New Haven, Conn.: Yale University Press, 1955), vol. 2, p. 68.

15. Note the emphasis, for example, placed in Elizabeth Dipple's assessment of Iris Murdoch's work: 'Good literature always evokes a serious response, an attention that involves more than aesthetic judgment. When we read a novel, we know we are looking at a version of life in which large issues affecting the basic way in which we view the world come into play; and when we judge a book to be good, we are saying quite a lot about ethical response as well as technique and form' (Elizabeth Dipple, *Iris Murdoch: Work for the Spirit* (Chicago, Ill.: University of Chicago Press, 1982) pp. 28–9).
16. Quoted in Adams, *Critical Theory Since Plato*.
17. Alexander Pope, 'An Essay on Criticism', quoted in ibid., p. 279.
18. Edmund Burke, 'A Philosophical Inquiry into the Origin of Our Ideas of the Sublime and Beautiful', in ibid., p. 303.
19. Ibid., p. 306.
20. William Wordsworth, 'Preface to the Second Edition of *Lyrical Ballads*', quoted in ibid., p. 435.
21. John Stuart Mill, 'What is Poetry?', quoted in ibid., p. 540.
22. Frank Lentricchia, *After the New Criticism* (Chicago, Ill.: University of Chicago Press, 1980) p. 241.
23. Richard Macksey, 'Velocities of Change', in Macksey (ed.), *Velocities of Change: Critical Essays from 'MLN'* (Baltimore, Md, and London: Johns Hopkins University Press, 1974) p. ix.
24. W.J. Harvey, *Character and the Novel* (Ithaca, N.Y.: Cornell University Press, 1965) p. 45.
25. Lentricchia, *After the New Criticism*, p. xiii.
26. Frank Burch Brown, *Transfiguration: Poetic Metaphor and the Languages of Religious Belief* (Chapel Hill, N.C.: University of North Carolina Press, 1983) p. 150.
27. Walter Slatoff, *With Respect to Readers: Dimensions of Literary Response* (Ithaca, N.Y.: Cornell University Press, 1970) p. 37.
28. M.H. Abrams, *The Mirror and the Lamp: Romantic Theory and the Critical Tradition* (New York: W.W. Norton, 1953), p. 272.
29. David C. Hoy, *The Critical Circle: Literature, History, and Philosophical Hermeneutics* (Berkeley, Cal.: University of California Press, 1978) p. 67.
30. Philip Wheelwright, *The Burning Fountain: A Study in the Language of Symbolism* (Bloomington, Ind.: Indiana University Press, 1968) pp. 18–19.
31. Jonathan Culler, *The Pursuit of Signs: Semiotics, Literature, Deconstruction* (Ithaca, N.Y.: Cornell University Press, 1981) p. ix.
32. Susanne Langer, *Philosophy in a New Key* (Cambridge, Mass.: Harvard University Press, 1959).
33. Abrams, *Mirror and the Lamp*, p. 22.
34. William K. Wimsatt, Jr and Cleanth Brooks, *Literary Criticism: A Short History* (New York: Random House, 1957) p. 371.
35. Abrams, *Mirror and the Lamp*, p. 65.
36. Wimsatt and Brooks, *Literary Criticism*, p. 370
37. Rene Wellek, *A History of Modern Criticism*, vol. 2: *The Romantic Age* (New Haven, Conn.: Yale University Press, 1955) p. 156.
38. Abrams, *Mirror and the Lamp*, p. 158.

39. Samuel Taylor Coleridge, *Collected Works*, vol. 7, pt 1: *Biographia Literaria*, ed. J. Engell and W.J. Bate (Princeton, N.J.: Princeton University Press, 1983) pp. 124–5.
40. Richard Harter Fogle, *The Idea of Coleridge's Criticism* (Berkeley, Cal.: University of California Press, 1962) p. 9.
41. Lentricchia, *After the New Criticism*, p. 13.
42. Kathleen Wheeler, 'Coleridge's Theory of Imagination: a Hegelian Solution to Kant?', in David Jasper (ed.), *The Interpretation of Belief: Coleridge, Schleiermacher and Romanticism* (London: Macmillan, 1986) esp. pp. 30ff.
43. S.T. Coleridge, *Collected Works*, vol. 6: *Lay Sermons*, ed. R.J. White (Princeton, N.J.: Princeton University Press, 1972), 'The Statesman's Manual', p. 30.
44. Ibid., vol. 7, pt 1, p. 304.
45. Wheelwright, *Burning Fountain*, p. 32.
46. Coleridge, *Collected Works*, vol. 7, pt 1, p. 305.
47. Wellek, *History of Modern Criticism*, vol. 2, pp. 185–6.
48. M.H. Abrams, *Natural Supernaturalism: Tradition and Revolution in Romantic Literature* (New York: W.W. Norton, 1971) p. 268.
49. Wellek, *History of Modern Criticism*, vol. 2, p. 170.
50. Coleridge, *Collected Works*, vol. 7, pt 2, pp. 16–17.
51. Abrams, *Mirror and the Lamp*, p. 171.
52. Fogle, *Idea of Coleridge's Criticism*, pp. 67–8.
53. Wheelwright, *Burning Fountain*, pp. 54–5.
54. See Jane P. Tompkins, 'The Reader in History: the Changing Shape of Literary Response', in *Reader-Response Criticism: From Formalism to Post-Structuralism*, ed. Jane P. Tompkins (Baltimore, Md: Johns Hopkins University Press, 1980) *passim*.
55. Vernon Ruland, *Horizons of Criticism: An Assessment of Religious–Literary Criticism* (Chicago, Ill.: American Library Association, 1975) p. 117.
56. Carl Jung, 'Psychology and Literature', in *The Spirit in Man, Art, and Literature*, trans. R.F.C. Hull (Princeton, N.J.: Princeton University Press, 1966) p. 85.
57. Maud Bodkin, *Archetypal Patterns in Poetry: Psychological Studies of Imagination* (1934; London: Oxford University Press, 1963).
58. Wimsatt and Brooks, *Literary Criticism*, pp. 716–20.
59. Aniela Jaffe, *The Myth of Meaning: Jung and the Expansion of Consciousness*, trans. R.F.C. Hull (New York: Penguin Books, 1975) pp. 15–16.
60. Edward F. Edinger, *Ego and Archetype: Individuation and the Religious Function of the Psyche* (New York: G.P. Putnam's Sons, 1972) p. 108.
61. Mark Schorer, *William Blake: The Politics of Vision* (New York: Holt, 1946) p. 29.
62. Richard Ellmann, *The Identity of Yeats* (New York: Oxford University Press, 1968).
63. Jung, 'Psychology and Literature', pp. 96–7.
64. Carl Jung, 'On the Relation of Analytical Psychology to Poetry', in *The*

Spirit in Man, Art, and Literature, trans. R.F.C. Hull (Princeton, N.J.: Princeton University Press, 1975) p. 85.
65. Ibid.
66. Jaffe, *Myth of Meaning*, p. 150.
67. Stanley Romaine Hopper, 'The Poetry of Meaning', in *Literature and Religion*, ed. Giles Gunn (New York: Harper & Row, 1971) p. 232.
68. Giles Gunn, 'American Literature and the Imagination of Otherness', in *Religion as Story*, ed. James B. Wiggins (New York: Harper & Row, 1975) p. 89.
69. Edinger, *Ego and Archetype*, p. 78.
70. Jaffe, *Myth of Meaning*, p. 37.
71. Jung, 'On the Relation...', p. 82.
72. Ibid., pp. 65–6.
73. Northrop Frye, *Anatomy of Criticism: Four Essays* (Princeton, N.J.: Princeton University Press, 1957) p. 88.
74. Ibid., p. 94.
75. Jaffe, *Myth of Meaning*, p. 68.
76. Wheelwright, *Burning Fountain*, p. 50.
77. Examples would include Martin Leonard Pops, *The Melville Archetype* (Kent, Ohio: Kent State University Press, 1970); Charles Fedelson's *Symbolism in American Literature* (Chicago, Ill.: University of Chicago Press, 1953); Robert Zoellner, *The Salt-Sea Mastodon: A Reading of 'Moby-Dick'* (Berkeley, Cal: University of California Press, 1973); Edwards Edinger's study, *Melville's Moby-Dick: A Jungian Commentary* (New York: New Directions, 1975), and scores of texts focusing on the significance generated by the language of *Ulysses*.
78. I shall mention for the nonce only one; it is recent, and certainly one of the best: Vincent B. Leitch, *American Literary Criticism from the Thirties to the Eighties* (New York: Columbia University Press, 1988).
79. Mary Annis Pratt, *Archetypal Patterns in Women's Fiction* (Bloomington, Ind.: Indiana University Press, 1981).

Notes to Chapter 3: Metaphysical Otherness

1. Paul Brodtkorb, *Ishmael's White World: A Phenomenological Reading of 'Moby Dick'* (New Haven, Conn.: Yale University Press, 1965) p. 82.
2. Edgar A. Dryden, *Melville's Thematics of Form: The Great Art of Telling the Truth* (Baltimore, Md.: Johns Hopkins University Press, 1968) p. 7.
3. R.W.B. Lewis, *The American Adam: Innocence, Tragedy and Tradition in the Nineteenth Century* (Chicago, Ill.: Chicago University Press, 1955) p. 131.
4. W.J. Harvey, *Character and the Novel* (Ithaca, N.Y.: Cornell University Press, 1968) p. 111.
5. Brodtkorb, *Ishmael's White World*, p. 148.
6. Richard H. Brodhead, *Hawthorne, Melville and the Novel* (Chicago, Ill.: University of Chicago Press, 1976) p. 162.
7. Richard Chase, *The American Novel and its Tradition* (Garden City, N.Y.: Doubleday Anchor Books, 1957) p. 100.

8. Ibid., p. 102.
9. A.N. Kaul, *The American Vision: Actual and Ideal Society in Nineteenth-Century Fiction* (New Haven, Conn.: Yale University Press, 1963) p. 258.
10. Giles Gunn, *The Interpretation of Otherness* (New York: Oxford University Press, 1979) p. 177.
11. Weslesy A. Kort, *Narrative Elements and Religious Meaning* (Philadelphia, Pa: Fortress Press, 1975) p. 36.
12. Hannah Arendt, quoted by Frank Kermode in his *The Sense of an Ending: Studies in the Theory of Fiction* (New York: Oxford University Press, 1967) p. 38.
13. Ibid., p. 166.
14. Langdon Gilkey, *Naming the Whirlwind: The Renewal of God-Language* (New York: Bobbs-Merrill, 1969) p. 253.
15. Gunn, *Interpretation of Otherness*, p. 223.
16. Gilkey, *Naming the Whirlwind*, p. 315.
17. Daniel Hoffman, *Form and Fable in American Fiction* (New York: Oxford University Press, 1965) p. 273.
18. Warwick Wadlington, *The Confidence Game in American Literature* (Princeton, N.J.: Princeton University Press, 1975) p. 97.
19. Edgar A. Dryden, *Melville's Thematics of Form: The Great Art of Telling the Truth* (Baltimore, Md: Johns Hopkins University Press, 1968) p. 7.
20. Hoffman, *Form and Fable in American Fiction*, p. 260.
21. Tony Tanner, *The Reign of Wonder: Naivety and Reality in American Literature* (New York: Harper & Row, 1965) p. 309.
22. A. Robert Lee, 'Moby Dick: the Tale and the Telling', in Faith Pullin (ed.), *New Perspectives on Melville* (Kent, Ohio: Kent State University Press, 1978) p. 114.
23. Tanner, *Reign of Wonder*, pp. 8–9.
24. Sallie TeSelle, *Literature and the Christian Life* (New Haven, Conn.: Yale University Press, 1966) p. 178.
25. Brodhead, *Hawthorne, Melville and the Novel*, p. 145.
26. Charles Feidelson, *Symbolism and American Literature* (Chicago, Ill.: University of Chicago Press, 1953) p. 183.
27. Maurice Friedman, *Problematic Rebel: Melville, Dostoievsky,, Kafka, Camus* (Chicago, Ill.: University of Chicago Press, 1970) p. 55.
28. John Seelye, *Melville: The Ironic Diagram* (Evanston, Ill.: Northwestern University Press, 1970) p. 64.
29. Bainard Cowan, *Exiled Waters: 'Moby-Dick' and the Crisis of Allegory* (Baton Rouge, and London: Louisiana State University Press, 1982) pp. 97–8.
30. Carolyn Porter, 'Call Me Ishmael, or How to Make Double-Talk Speak', in Richard H. Brodhead (ed.), *New Essays on 'Moby-Dick'* (Cambridge: Cambridge University Press, 1986), p. 74.
31. Seelye, *Melville*, p. 4.
32. William Hamilton, *Melville and the Gods* (Chico, Cal.: Scholars Press, 1985) p. 68.
33. Chase, *American Novel*, pp. 91–2.
34. Friedman, *Problematic Rebel*, p. 68.

35. Hoffman, *Form and Fable*, p. 240.
36. Brodhead, *Hawthorne, Melville and the Novel*, p. 146.
37. Merlin Bowen, *The Long Encounter: Self and Experience in the Writings of Herman Melville* (Chicago, Ill.: University of Chicago Press, 1960) p. 135.
38. Brodhead, *Hawthorne, Melville and the Novel*, pp. 161–2.
39. Lewis, *American Adam*, p. 130.
40. Friedman, *Problematic Rebel*, pp. 68–9.
41. Tanner, *Reign of Wonder*, pp. 355, 356.
42. See Tony Tanner, *The Reign of Wonder: Naivety and Reality in American Literature* (New York: Harper & Row, 1965) p. 8.
43. Lewis, *American Adam*, p. 132.
44. Nathan A. Scott, Jr, *The Broken Center: Studies in the Theological Horizon of Modern Literature* (New Haven, Conn.: Yale University Press, 1966), pp. 123, 131.
45. William B. Dillingham, *Melville's Later Novels* (Athens, Ga, and London: University of Georgia Press, 1986) p. 143.
46. Brodhead, *Hawthorne, Melville and the Novel*, p. 161.
47. Seelye, *Melville*, p. 6.
48. Bert Bender, 'Moby-Dick: an American Lyrical Novel', *Studies in the Novel*, 10 (Fall 1978) p. 354.
49. Hoffman, *Form and Fable*, p. 273.
50. Marius Bewley, *The Eccentric Design: Form in the Classic American Novel* (New York: Columbia University Press, 1963) p. 205.

Notes to Chapter 4: Epiphanic Otherness

1. Marilyn French, *The Book as World: James Joyce's 'Ulysses'* (Cambridge, Mass.: Harvard University Press, 1976) p. 4.
2. Richard Ellmann, *Ulysses on the Liffey* (New York: Oxford University Press, 1972) p. 43.
3. Robert Langbaum, 'The Epiphanic Mode in Wordsworth and Modern Literature', *New Literary History*, 14 (Winter 1983) p. 351.
4. Robert K. Martin, *Hero, Captain, and Stranger: Male Friendship, Social Critique, and Literary Form in the Sea Novels of Herman Melville* (Chapel Hill, N.C., and London: University of North Carolina Press, 1986) p. 94.
5. Robert Scholes, *Structuralism in Literature: An Introduction* (New Haven, Conn.: Yale University Press, 1974) p. 192.
6. M.H. Abrams, *Natural Supernaturalism: Tradition and Revolution in Romantic Literature* (New York: W.W. Norton, 1971) p. 421.
7. Robert Scholes, 'Joyce and the Epiphany: the Key to the Labyrinth?', *Sewanee Review*, 72 (Winter 1964) p. 73.
8. Richard Ellmann, *James Joyce* (New York: Oxford University Press, 1959) p. 89.
9. These three adjectives continue to be favourites of Nathan Scott and may be found throughout his writings, especially when he is detailing his own sacramental theology; see, for example, his *The Wild Prayer of*

Longing: Poetry and the Sacred (New Haven, Conn., and London: Yale University Press, 1971) and *The Poetics of Belief* (Chapel Hill, N.C.: University of North Carolina Press, 1985) passim.
10. James Joyce, *Stephen Hero*, ed. Theodore Spencer, rev. John J. Slocum and Herbert Cahoon (Norfolk, Conn.: New Directions, 1963) p. 213.
11. Morris Beja, *Epiphany and the Modern Novel* (Seattle, Wash.: University of Washington Press, 1971) p. 18.
12. S.L. Goldberg, *The Classical Temper* (New York: Barnes & Noble, 1961) p. 223.
13. Stanley Romaine Hopper, 'The Poetry of Meaning', in Giles Gunn (ed.), *Literature and Religion* (New York: Harper & Row, 1971) p. 227.
14. Anthony Burgess, *Re Joyce* (New York: Ballantine Books, 1965) p. 28.
15. Hopper, 'Poetry of Meaning', p. 229.
16. Iris Murdoch, *The Sovereignty of Good* (New York: Schocken Books, 1971) p. 65.
17. Goldberg, *Classical Temper*, p. 253.
18. Giles Gunn, 'American Literature and the Imagination of Otherness', in James B. Wiggins (ed.), *Religion as Story* (New York: Harper & Row, 1975) p. 89.
19. David Hayman, *'Ulysses': The Mechanics of Meaning* (Madison, Wis.: University of Wisconsin Press, 1982) p. 129.
20. Jon Lanham, 'The Genre of *A Portrait of the Artist as a Young Man* and "the Rhythm of its Structure" ', Genre, 10 (Spring 1977) p. 93.
21. Brian Wicker, *The Story-Shaped World: Fiction and Metaphysics: Some Variations on a Theme* (Notre Dame, Ind.: University of Notre Dame Press, 1975) p. 101.
22. Hayman, *'Ulysses'* p. 22.
23. Michal Groden, *'Ulysses' in Progress* (Princeton, N.J.: Princeton University Press, 1977) pp. 50–1.
24. Scholes, *Structuralism*, p. 187.
25. Wolfang Iser, *The Implied Reader* (Baltimore, Md: Johns Hopkins University Press, 1974) p. 183.
26. Gerald L. Bruns, 'Eumaeus', in Clive Hart and David Hayman (eds), *James Joyce's 'Ulysses': Critical Essays* (Berkeley, Cal.: University of California Press, 1974) p. 363.
27. Maurice Natanson, *Literature, Philosophy and the Social Sciences: Essays in Existentialism and Phenomenology* (The Hague: Martinus Nijhoff, 1968) p. 132.
28. Robert Scholes and Robert Kellogg, *The Nature of Narrative* (New York: Oxford University Press, 1966) p. 128.
29. French, *Book as World*, p. 214.
30. The phrase is translated and used by Joseph Kestner in his article 'Virtual Text/Virtual Reader: the Structural Signature Within, Behind, Beyond, Above', *James Joyce Quarterly*, 16 (Fall 1978/Winter 1979) p. 37.
31. Hugh Kenner, *Joyce's Voices* (Berkeley, Cal.: University of California Press, 1978) p. 38.

32. Ellmann, *Ulysses on the Liffey*, p. 97.
33. Richard M. Kain, *Fabulous Voyager* (Chicago, Ill.: University of Chicago Press, 1947) p. 85.
34. Karen Lawrence writes: 'The eloquence of the writing and the significance of the drama are deflated: both style and climax are revealed to be clichés – one linguistic, the other dramatic. And yet, somehow, by "sacrificing" the moment of climax, Joyce gets something back. The clichéd writing is an artistic strategy to allow emotion and articulate eloquence to enter the narrative obliquely. In language that deliberately claims very little, he finds a way to suggest emotion while avoiding sentimentality, and significance while avoiding dramatic climax. Somehow the very lameness and incompetence of the writing creates the proper significance of the moment of meeting' (Lawrence, *The Odyssey of Style in 'Ulysses'* (Princeton, N.J.: Princeton University Press, 1980) pp. 177–8.
35. James Joyce, *Ulysses: The Corrected Text*, ed. Hans Walter Gabler with Wolfhard Steppe and Claus Melchior (New York: Random House, 1986) p. 502. Throughout the chapter, pagination of this most adequate of all possible editions will be parenthetically included in the text, directly following quotes, prefaced by the symbol 'U'.
36. Burgess, *Re Joyce*, p. 215.
37. Ellmann, *James Joyce*, p. 88.
38. Iser, *Implied Reader*, p. 191.
39. Scholes and Kellogg, *Nature of Narrative*, p. 257.
40. Ellmann, *Ulysses on the Liffey*, p. xvi.
41. Jonathan Culler, *The Pursuit of Signs* (Ithaca, N.Y.: Cornell University Press, 1981) p. 54.
42. James H. Maddox, *Joyce's 'Ulysses' and the Assault upon Character* (New Brunswick, N.J.: Rutgers University Press, 1978) p. 8.
43. Charles Rossman, 'The Reader's Role in *A Portrait of the Artist as a Young Man'*, in Suheil Badi Bushrui and Bernard Benstock (eds), *James Joyce: An International Perspective* (Totawa, N.J.: Barnes & Nobel, 1982) p. 25.
44. Brook Thomas, 'Not a Reading *of*, but the Act of Reading "*Ulysses*" ', *James Joyce Quaterly*, 16 (Fall 1978/Winter 1979) p. 84.
45. Brook Thomas, 'The Counterfeit Style of "Eumaeus" ', *James Joyce Quarterly*, 14 (Fall 1976) p. 21.
46. Bruns, 'Eumaeus', p. 369.
47. Maddox, *Joyce's 'Ulysses'*, p. 17.
48. Wolfgang Iser, *The Act of Reading* (Baltimore, Md: Johns Hopkins University Press, 1977) p. 15.
49. Groden, *'Ulysses' in Progress*, p. 32.
50. French, *Book as World*, p. 17.
51. Iser, *The Implied Reader*, p. 192.
52. Ibid., p. 225.
53. French, *Book as World*, p. 215.
54. Robert Magliola, *Phenomenology and Literature: An Introduction* (West Lafayette, Ind.: Purdue University Press, 1977) p. 67.

Notes to Chapter 5: Hermeneutic Otherness

1. Genevieve Lloyd, 'Iris Murdoch on the Ethical Significance of Truth', *Philosophy and Literature*, 6 (1982) p. 74.
2. Geoffrey Hartman, *Criticism in the Wilderness* (New Haven, Conn.: Yale University Press, 1980) p. 37.
3. Fredric Jameson, *The Political Unconscious* (Ithaca, N.Y.: Cornell University Press, 1981) p. 77.
4. Hartman, *Criticism in the Wilderness*, p. 68.
5. David Couzens Hoy, *The Critical Circle* (Berkeley, Cal.: University of California Press, 1978) p. 48.
6. Vladimir Nabokov, *Lectures on Literature*, ed. Fredson Bowers (New York: Harcourt, Brace, Jovanovich, 1980) p. 3.
7. Iris Murdoch, *The Black Prince* (New York: Viking Press, 1973) pp. 55–6.
8. Elizabeth Dipple, *Iris Murdoch: Work for the Spirit* (Chicago, Ill.: University of Chicago Press, 1982) p. 87.
9. Robert Scholes, *Structuralism in Literature* (New Haven, Conn.: Yale University Press, 1974) p. 173.
10. Ibid., p. 178
11. Ibid., p. 181.
12. Ibid., p. 197.
13. Iris Murdoch, 'The Sublime and the Good', *Chicago Review* (Autumn 1959) p. 49.
14. Iris Murdoch, *The Book and the Brotherhood* (New York: Viking Penguin, 1988) p. 172.
15. Murdoch's most recent novel, *The Message to the Planet* (New York: Viking Penguin, 1990), is, like the two previous narratives, told in the third person.
16. Ibid., p. 32.
17. Edward Said, *Beginnings: Intention and Method* (Baltimore, Md: Johns Hopkins University Press, 1975) pp. 144–5.
18. Murdoch, *Black Prince*, p. 11.
19. Hans Robert Jauss, *Toward an Aesthetics of Reception*, trans. Timothy Bahti (Minneapolis, Minn.: University of Minnesota Press, 1982) p. 41.
20. Iris Murdoch, *The Sovereignty of Good* (New York: Schocken Books, 1971) pp. 74–5.
21. Nathan A. Scott, Jr, *Three American Moralists* (Notre Dame, Ind.: University of Notre Dame Press, 1973) p. 54.
22. This familiar phrase is still employed readily to characterise the method of New Criticism. Roger Shattuck, for example, speaks of its pedagogy as 'sustained attention to "the text itself" '. See Shattuck, 'The State of Criticism', *Partisan Review*, 47 (1980) p. 440.
23. Dipple, *Iris Murdoch*, p. 46.
24. It is evident that a host of critics is engaged in all manner of discourse about, as Roger Shattuck has expressed it, the nature of the power of literature 'to convey a sense of *otherness*, to let us enter another person's thought, to allow us to get out of our own skin' (see Shattuck, 'State of Criticism', p. 441).

25. Hans Robert Jauss, 'Literary History as a Challenge to Literary Theory', in Ralph Cohen (ed.), *New Directions in Literary History* (Baltimore, Md: Johns Hopkins University Press, 1974) p. 19.
26. Wolfgang Iser, *The Implied Reader* (Baltimore, Md.: Johns Hopkins University Press, 1974) p. 275.
27. Ibid., p. 279.
28. Iris Murdoch, 'Against Dryness', *Encounter*, 16 (1961) p. 20.
29. Ibid., p. 18.
30. Ibid., p. 19.
31. Frank Kermode, 'House of Fiction: Interviews with Seven English Novelists', in Malcolm Bradbury (ed.), *The Novel Today: Contemporary Writers on Modern Fiction* (Manchester: University of Manchester Press, 1977) p. 114.
32. Peter J. Conradi, *Iris Murdoch: The Saint and the Artist*, 2nd edn (London: Macmillan Press, 1989) p. ix.
33. Murdoch, *Sovereignty of Good*, p. 88.
34. Dipple, *Iris Murdoch*, p. 78.
35. Frank Baldanza, 'Iris Murdoch and the Theory of Personality', *Criticism*, 7 (Spring 1965) p. 178.
36. Sharon Kaehele and Howard German, 'The Discovery of Reality in Iris Murdoch's *The Bell*', *PMLA*, 82 (December 1967) p. 562.
37. Northrop Frye, 'The Road of Excess', in B. Slote (ed.), *Myth and Symbol: Critical Approaches and Applications* (Lincoln, Neb.: University of Nebraska Press, 1984) p. 14.
38. Iser, *Implied Reader*, p. 290.
39. Robert Scholes and Robert Kellogg, *The Nature of Narrative* (New York: Oxford University Press, 1966) p. 240.
40. Ibid., pp. 256, 263.
41. M.H. Abrams, *A Glossary of Literary Terms*, 3rd edn (New York: Holt, Rinehart & Winston, 1971) pp. 81–2.
42. Iris Murdoch, *A Severed Head* (New York: Viking Press, 1961). As instanced at this point in the chapter, pagination will be included in the text, and will be preceded by the abbreviation '*SH*'.
43. Jonathan Culler, *Structuralist Poetics: Structuralism, Linguistics, and the Study of Literature* (Ithaca, N.Y.: Cornell University Press, 1975) p. 157.
44. Scholes, *Structuralism*, p. 147.
45. Conradi, *Iris Murdoch*, p. 32.
46. Wolfgang Iser, *The Act of Reading* (Baltimore, Md: Johns Hopkins University Press, 1978) p. 43.
47. Iser, *Implied Reader*, pp. 281–2.
48. Scholes and Kellogg, *Nature of Narrative*, p. 256.
49. See Paul B. Armstrong, 'Part II. Conradian Bewilderment: the Metaphysics of Belief', in his *The Challenge of Bewilderment: Understanding and Representation in James, Conrad, and Ford* (Ithaca, N.Y.: Cornell University Press, 1987) pp. 107–85.
50. Murdoch, *Sovereignty of Good*, p. 87.
51. Robert Scholes, *The Fabulators* (New York: Oxford University Press, 1967) p. 108.

52. Wayne Booth, *The Rhetoric of Irony* (Chicago, Ill.: University of Chicago Press, 1974).
53. Harold Toliver, *Animate Illusions: Explorations of Narrative Structure* (Lincoln, Neb.: University of Nebraska Press, 1974) p. 93.
54. Ibid., p. 96.
55. Alice P. Kenny, 'The Mythic History of *A Severed Head*', *Modern Fiction Studies*, 15 (Autumn 1969) p. 387.
56. Ibid., p. 398.
57. Robert R. Magliola, *Phenomenology and Literature: An Introduction* (West Lafayette, Ind.: Purdue University Press, 1977) p. 120.
58. Richard Palmer, *Hermeneutics: Interpretation Theory in Schleiermacher, Dilthey, Heidegger and Gadamer* (Evanston, Ill.: Northwestern University Press, 1966) p. 233.
59. Jane P. Tompkins describes a moral note in Iser's work: 'Iser's position extends the field of critical activity to include not only a new subject matter – the phenomenology of the reading process – but also a new moral emphasis. [H]e views the application of his insights as therapeutic, leading to fuller knowledge of the self and even to self-creation.' See Jane P. Tompkins (ed.), *Reader-Response Criticism: From Formalism to Post-Structuralism* (Baltimore, Md, and London: Johns Hopkins University Press, 1980) p. xv. Kuenzli furthers this same focus on 'the fuller knowledge of the self' in his review of Iser's *The Act of Reading* when he writes: 'The extent of the reader's activity in reading depends on the degree to which the text confirms or distorts the reader's familiar norms. The function of literature is therefore to question and invalidate the thought systems which it has chosen for its repertoire. This deautomatization of conventions has as its goal to "rearrange existing patterns of meaning". The repertoire invoked is the meeting ground between text and reader, but the text's strategic violation of traditional social, cultural, and literary norms disorients and restructures the reader's comprehension of the familiar. Only through a fictive work that suspends the reader's accustomed relationship with the work, can he recognize the limitations and deficiencies of traditional codes and norms.' See Rudolf E. Kuenzli, 'The Intersubjective Structure of the Reading Process: a Cummunication-Orientated Theory of Literature', *Diacritics*, 10 (June 1980) pp. 50–1.
60. Palmer, *Hermeneutics*, p. 234.
61. James Gindin, 'Images of Illusion in the Work of Iris Murdoch', *Texas Studies in Literature and Language*, 2 (Summer 1960) p. 186. It should be noted that although this essay was written before *A Severed Head* was published, its relevance still obtains.
62. Dipple, *Iris Murdoch*, p. 97.
63. Iris Murdoch, *The Sea, The Sea* (New York: Viking Press, 1978; Penguin Books, 1980). A brief example from page 63: 'Rereading these paragraphs I feel again that I am giving the wrong impression. What a difficult form autobiography is proving to be!'
64. Giles B. Gunn, *The Interpretation of Otherness: Literature, Religion and the American Imagination* (New York: Oxford University Press) p. 90.
65. Conradi, in his throughly engaging work, notes that 'Murdoch's

extraordinary skill at ambushing the reader's expectations' serves her concern 'to redirect the reader's attention to the sensory world in which he is immersed', a late world, she believes, now of 'unhoused spirituality'. See Conradi, *Iris Murdoch*, pp. 92, 48, 134.
66. Gunn, *Interpretation of Otherness*, p. 103.

Notes to Chapter 6: Conclusion

1. J. Hillis Miller, Presidential Address, 1986: 'The Triumph of Theory, the Resistance to Reading, and the Question of the Material Base', *PMLA*, 102 (3) (May 1987) p. 281.
2. Tony Tanner, *Adultery in the Novel: Contract and Trangression* (Baltimore, Md, and London: Johns Hopkins University Press, 1979) p. 90.
3. Wayne Booth, *The Company We Keep: An Ethics of Fiction* (Berkeley, Cal.: University of California Press, 1988) p. 6.
4. Margaret Atwood, 'Northrop Frye Observed', in *Second Words* (Boston, Mass.: Beacon Press, 1984) p. 405.
5. A method surely not alien to the current enterprise of practical criticism, I should add; Jonathan Arac speaks of Frank Kermode's posture as one of 'fruitful eclecticism', for example. See Arac, *Critical Genealogies: Historical Situations for Postmodern Literary Studies* (New York: Columbia University Press, 1987) p. 223.
6. Giles Gunn, *The Interpretation of Otherness* (New York: Oxford University Press, 1979) p. 5.
7. Although this phrase is taken from Wolfgang Iser's book of 1978, *The Act of Reading* (Baltimore, Md, and London: Johns Hopkins University Press), it expresses aptly his current concerns; see his recently published *Prospecting: From Reader Response to Literary Anthropology* (Baltimore, Md, and London: Johns Hopkins University Press, 1989).
8. Edward Said, *Beginnings: Intention and Method* (Baltimore, Md: Johns Hopkins University Press, 1975) pp. 144–5.
9. Robert Detweiler (ed.), *Art/Literature/Religion: Life on the Borders*, American Academy of Religion Thematic Studies no. 49/2 (Chico, Cal.: Scholars Press, 1982).
10. J. Hillis Miller, *The Ethics of Reading* (New York: Columbia University Press, 1987)
11. Terry Eagleton, *Literary Theory* (Minneapolis, Minn.: University of Minnesota Press, 1983) p. 65.
12. Miller, Presidential Address 1986, p. 282.
13. Nathan A. Scott, Jr, *The Poetics of Belief* (Chapel Hill, N.C.: University of North Carolina Press, 1985) p. 129.
14. Miller, Presidential Address 1986, p. 283.
15. Lynn M. Poland, *Literary Criticism and Biblical Hermeneutics: A Critique of Formalist Approaches* (Chico, Cal.: Scholars Press, 1985) pp. 169–70.
16. Wolfgang Iser, 'Towards a Literary Anthropology', in Ralph Cohen (ed.), *The Future of Literary Theory* (New York and London: Routledge, Chapman and Hall, 1989) p. 228.
17. Ibid. See also David Miller's discussion of such liminality in the inter-

chapter, 'Interlude: Liminality, Boundary, and the Between', in David L. Miller, *Three Faces of God: Traces of the Trinity in Literature and Life* (Philadelphia, Pa: Fortress Press, 1986) pp. 65–79.
18. Robin Feuer Miller, *Dostoevsky and 'The Idiot': Author, Narrator, and Reader* (Cambridge, Mass., and London: Harvard University Press, 1981).
19. Brook Thomas, *James Joyce's 'Ulysses': A Book of Many Happy Returns* (Baton Rouge, La, and London: Louisiana State University Press, 1982).
20. Warwick Wadlington, *Reading Faulknerian Tragedy* (Ithaca, N.Y., and London: Cornell University Press, 1987) p. 15.
21. Wolfgang Iser, 'Towards a Literary Anthropology', in Ralph Cohen (ed.), *The Future of Literary Theory* (New York and London: Routledge, Chapman and Hall, 1989), pp. 216–17.
22. Martin Price, *Forms of Life* (New Haven, Conn.: Yale University Press, 1983) p. 6.
23. Booth, *The Company We Keep*, pp. 38–9.
24. Ibid., p. 56.
25. Ibid., p. 60.
26. Ibid., p. 62.
27. Ibid., p. 64.
28. Ibid., p. 69.
29. Ibid., p. 70.
30. Ibid., p. 88.
31. Ibid., pp. 194–5.
32. Wesley Kort, *Modern Fiction and Human Time: A Study in Narrative and Belief* (Tampa, Fla: University Presses of Florida/University of South Florida Press, 1985) p. 173.
33. Geoffrey Hartman, *Criticism in the Wilderness: The Study of Literature Today* (New Haven, Conn.: Yale University Press, 1980) pp. 89–90.
34. Frank Lentricchia, *After the New Criticism* (Chicago, Ill.: University of Chicago Press, 1980) pp. 8–9.
35. Northrop Frye, *Anatomy of Criticism: Four Essays* (Princeton, N.J.: Princeton University Press, 1957); pagination of this book will be included in the text and preceded by 'AC'.
36. Robert Langbaum, *The Modern Spirit: Essays on the Continuity of Nineteenth- and Twentieth-Century Literature* (New York: Oxford University Press, 1970) p. 10.
37. Lentricchia, *After the New Criticism*, p. 23.
38. Ibid., p. 15.
39. Justus George Lawler, *Celestial Pantomime: Poetic Structures of Transcendence* (New Haven, Conn.: Yale University Press, 1979) pp. 21–2.
40. Walter Benn Michaels, 'The Interpreter's Self', *Georgia Review*, 31 (Summer 1977) pp. 383, 385.
41. See Jane P. Tompkins, 'The Reader in History', in Jane P. Tompkins (ed.), *Reader-Response Criticism* (Baltimore, Md: Johns Hopkins University Press, 1980) pp. 201–32.
42. Richard Poirier, *The Renewal of Literature: Emersonian Reflections* (New York: Random House, 1987) pp. 100–1.

43. Wolfgang Iser, *The Act of Reading* (Baltimore, Md: Johns Hopkins University Press, 1978) p. 10.
44. Jonathan Culler, *Structuralist Poetics* (Ithaca, N.Y.: Cornell University Press, 1975) p. 123.
45. William Ray, *Literary Meaning: From Phenomenology to Deconstruction* (Oxford: Basil Blackwell, 1984) p. 33.
46. Susan Suleiman, 'Introduction: Varieties of Audience-Oriented Criticism', in Susan Suleiman and Inge Crosman (eds), *The Reader in the Text* (Baltimore, Md: Johns Hopkins University Press, 1980) pp. 3–45.
47. David Couzens Hoy, *The Critical Circle* (Berkeley, Cal.: University of California Press, 1978) p. 67.
48. Gunn, *Interpretation of Otherness*, p. 124.
49. A familiar attitude: Wellek's presentation, 'The Mode of Existence of the Literary Work at Art', in Rene Wellek and Austin Warren, *Theory of Literature*, 3rd edn (New York: Harcourt Brace & World, 1956) is informed by Ingarden's understanding of the literary text.
50. Rudolph Kuenzli, 'The Intersubjective Structure of the Reading Process: a Communication-Oriented Theory of Literature', *Diacritics*, 10 (June 1980) p. 50.
51. Steven Mailloux, *Interpretive Conventions* (Ithaca, N.Y.: Cornell University Press, 1982) p. 44.
52. Jonathan Culler, *On Deconstruction* (Ithaca, N.Y.: Cornell University Press, 1982) p. 38.
53. Iser, *Act of Reading*, p. 15.
54. Culler, *On Deconstruction*, p. 72.
55. See 'Political Criticism: Confronting Religion', in Jonathan Culler, *Framing the Sign: Criticism and Its Institutions* (Norman, Okla, and London: University of Oklahoma Press, 1988) pp. 69–82.
56. M.H. Abrams continues to serve as ballast for the forays of Miller, though Abrams's impassioned pleas function more basically, I think, to point up Miller's activity as literary critical gadfly 'guest' to Abrams's 'host'. See the several discussions of Miller in M.H. Abrams, *Doing Things with Texts: Essays in Criticism and Critical Theory*, ed. Michael Fischer (New York: W.W. Norton, 1989) passim.
57. J. Hillis Miller, *The Times Literary Supplement*, no. 4410 (9–15 October 1987) p. 1104.
58. Richard Wentz, *The Contemplation of Otherness* (Macon, Ga: Mercer University Press, 1984) p. 11.
59. William Desmond, *Desire, Dialectic and Otherness: An Essay on Origins* (New Haven, Conn., and London: Yale University Press, 1987) p. 1.
60. Joanne Frye, *Living Stories, Telling Lives: Women and the Novel in Contemporary Experience* (Ann Arbor, Mich.: University of Michigan Press, 1986) p. 200.
61. To use a phrase found in 'The Sunrise', the penultimate tale of Margaret Atwood's *Bluebeard's Egg* (Boston, Mass.: Houghton Mifflin, 1986).
62. Iser, *Act of Reading*, p. 167.
63. Harold Bloom, *Ruin the Sacred Truths: Poetry and Belief from the Bible to*

the Present (Cambridge, Mass., and London: Harvard University Press, 1989) p. 133.
64. Hayden White, *Tropics of Discourse* (Baltimore, Md: Johns Hopkins University Press, 1978) p. 51.
65. Wallace Stevens, 'Notes Towards a Supreme Fiction', in *The Collected Poems of Wallace Stevens* (New York: Alfred A. Knopf, 1954).

Select Bibliography

Abrams, Meyer H., *Doing Things with Texts: Essays in Criticism and Critical Theory*, ed. Michael Fischer (New York: W.W. Norton, 1989).

―――, *Natural Supernaturalism: Tradition and Revolution in Romantic Literature* (New York: W.W. Norton, 1971).

Adams, Hazard (ed.), *Critical Theory Since Plato* (New York: Harcourt Brace Jovanovich, 1971).

Beja, Morris, *Epiphany and the Modern Novel* (Seattle, Wash.: University of Washington Press, 1971).

Bloom, Harold, *Ruin the Sacred Truths: Poetry and Belief from the Bible to the Present* (Cambridge, Mass.: Harvard University Press, 1989).

Booth, Wayne, *The Company We Keep: An Ethics of Fiction* (Berkeley, Cal.: University of California Press, 1988).

Brodtkorb, Paul, *Ishmael's White World* (New Haven, Conn.: Yale University Press, 1965).

Brown, Frank Burch, *Transfiguration: Poetic Metaphor and the Languages of Religious Belief* (Chapel Hill, N.C.: University of North Carolina Press, 1983).

Cohen, Ralph (ed.), *The Future of Literary Theory* (New York and London: Routledge, Chapman and Hall, 1989).

Conradi, Peter J., *Iris Murdoch: The Saint and the Artist*, 2nd edn (London: Macmillan Press, 1989).

Cowan, Bainard, *Exiled Waters: 'Moby-Dick' and the Crisis of Allegory* (Baton Rouge, La, and London: Louisiana State University Press, 1982).

Culler, Jonathan, *The Pursuit of Signs: Semiotics, Literature, Deconstruction* (Ithaca, N.Y.: Cornell University Press, 1981).

Desmond, William, *Desire, Dialectic and Otherness: An Essay on Origins* (New Haven, Conn.: Yale University Press, 1987).

Detweiler, Robert, *Breaking the Fall: Religious Readings of Contemporary Fiction* (New York: Harper & Row, 1989).

Dipple, Elizabeth, *Iris Murdoch: Work for Spirit* (Chicago, Ill.: University of Chicago Press, 1982).

Dryden, Edgar, *Melville's Thematics of Form: The Great Art of Telling the Truth* (Baltimore, Md: Johns Hopkins University Press, 1968).

Eagleton, Terry, *The Ideology of the Aesthetic* (Cambridge, Mass.: Basil Blackwell, 1990).

―――, *Literary Theory* (Minneapolis, Minn.: University of Minnesota Press, 1983).

Ford, Marcus Peter, *William James's Philosophy* (Amherst, Mass.: University of Massachusetts Press, 1982).

Gilkey, Langdon, *Naming the Whirlwind: The Renewal of God-Language* (New York: Bobbs-Merrill, 1969).

Graff, Gerald, *Literature against Itself: Literary Ideas in Modern Society* (Chicago, Ill.: University of Chicago Press, 1979).

Gunn, Giles, *The Culture of Criticism and the Criticism of Culture* (New York: Oxford University Press, 1987).
_____, *The Interpretation of Otherness: Literature, Religion, and the American Imagination* (New York: Oxford University Press, 1979).
Hartman, Geoffrey, *Criticism in the Wilderness: The Study of Literature Today* (New Haven, Conn.: Yale University Press, 1980).
Harvey, W.J. *Character and the Novel* (Ithaca, N.Y.: Cornell University Press, 1965).
Hoy, David Couzens, *The Critical Circle* (Berkeley, Cal.: University of California Press, 1978).
Iser, Wolfgang, *The Act of Reading* (Baltimore, Md, and London: Johns Hopkins University Press, 1978).
_____, *Prospecting: From Reader Response to Literary Anthropology* (Baltimore, Md, and London: Johns Hopkins University Press, 1989).
Jameson, Fredric, *The Political Unconscious* (Ithaca, N.Y. Cornell University Press, 1981).
Jasper, David, *The Study of Literature and Religion* (London: Macmillan, 1989).
_____ (ed.), *Images of Belief in Literature* (New York: St Martin's Press, 1984).
Jauss, Hans Robert, *Toward an Aesthetics of Reception*, trans. Timothy Bahti (Minneapolis, Minn.: University of Minnesota Press, 1982).
Josipovici, Gabriel, *The Book of God: A Response to the Bible* (New Haven, Conn.: Yale University Press, 1988).
Kort, Wesley, *Modern Fiction and Human Time: A Study in Narrative and Belief* (Tampa, Fla.: University Presses of Florida/University of South Florida Press, 1985).
_____, *Narrative Elements and Religious Meaning* (Philadelphia, Pa: Fortress Press, 1975).
Letich, Vincent B., *American Literary Criticism from the Thirties to the Eighties* (New York: Columbia University Press, 1988).
Lentricchia, Frank, *After the New Criticism* (Chicago, Ill.: University of Chicago Press, 1980).
Magliola, Robert R., *Phenomenology and Literature: An Introduction* (West Lafayette, Ind.: Purdue University Press, 1977).
Mailloux, Stephen, *Interpretive Conventions* (Ithaca, N.Y.: Cornell University Press, 1982).
Miller, David L., *Three Faces of God: Traces of the Trinity in Literature and Life* (Philadelphia, Pa: Fortress Press, 1986).
Miller, J. Hillis, *The Ethics of Reading* (New York: Columbia University Press, 1987).
Murdoch, Iris, *The Sovereignty of Good* (New York: Schocken Books, 1971).
Natanson, Maurice, *Literature, Philosophy and the Social Sciences* (The Hague: Martinus Nijhoff, 1968).
Palmer, Richard, *Hermeneutics: Interpretation Theory in Schleiermacher, Dilthey, Heidegger and Gadamer* (Evanston, Ill.: Northwestern University Press, 1966).
Price, Martin, *Forms of Life* (New Haven, Conn.: Yale University Press, 1983).

Select Bibliography

Rabinowitz, Peter J., *Before Reading: Narrative Conventions and the Politics of Interpretation* (Ithaca, N.Y.: Cornell University Press, 1987).
Said, Edward, *Beginnings: Intention and Method* (Baltimore, Md: Johns Hopkins University Press, 1975).
Scholes, Robert, *Structuralism in Literature: An Introduction* (New Haven, Conn.: Yale University Press, 1974).
Scott, Nathan A., Jr, *The Poetics of Belief* (Chapel Hill, N.C.: University of North Carolina Press, 1985).
Siebers, Tobin, *The Ethics of Criticism* (Ithaca, N.Y.: Cornell University Press, 1988).
Steiner, George, *Real Presences* (London: Faber & Faber, 1989).
Suleiman, Susan and Crosman, Inge, (eds), *The Reader in the Text* (Princeton, N.J.: Princeton University Press, 1980).
Tanner, Tony, *The Reign of Wonder: Naivety and Reality in American Literature* (New York: Harper & Row, 1965).
Tompkins, Jane P. (ed.), *Reader-Response Criticism: From Formalism to Post-Structuralism* (Baltimore, Md, and London: Johns Hopkins University Press, 1980).
Turner, Victor, *The Ritual Process* (Ithaca, N.Y.: Cornell University Press, 1969).
Wadlington, Warwick, *Reading Faulknerian Tragedy* (Ithaca, N.Y., and London: Cornell University Press, 1987).
Wentz, Richard, *The Contemplation of Otherness* (Macon, Ga: Mercer University Press, 1987).
Wheelwright, Philip, *The Burning Fountain: A Study in the Language of Symbolism* (Bloomington, Ind.: Indiana University Press, 1954).
White, Hayden, *Tropics of Discourse* (Baltimore, Md: Johns Hopkins University Press, 1978).
Wicker, Brian, *The Story-Shaped World: Fiction and Metaphysics* (Notre Dame, Ind.: University of Notre Dame Press, 1975).
Wimmers, Inge Crosman, *Poetics of Reading: Approaches to the Novel* (Princeton, N.J.: Princeton University Press, 1988).

Index

Abrams, M. H. 20, 21–2, 66, 99, 118, 121, 136
Archetypal criticism 4, 32, 33–4, 38
Arendt, Hannah 44
Aristotle 12–13
Atwood, Margaret 118

Baldanza, Frank 96
Beja, Morris 67
Bender, Bert 62
Bewley, Maurice 62
Bodkin, Maud 32
Booth, Wayne 110, 118, 122–4
Bowen, Merlin 57
Brodhead, Richard 42, 57
Brodtkorb, Paul 5, 40, 41
Brown, Frank Burch 18
Bruns, Gerald 73
Burgess, Anthony 69

Chase, Richard 56
Coleridge, Samuel Taylor 4, 11, 19–20, 23–9
Culler, Jonathan 6, 20, 83, 136

Detweiler, Robert 119
Dipple, Elizabeth 96, 114–15

Edinger, Edward 34, 37
Eliot, T. S. 18, 31
Ellmann, Richard 34, 66, 81, 86
Epiphany 64, 82, 83, 87–8
Epiphany, in modern literature 6, 64
Epiphany, Joyce's theory of 5–6, 65, 66, 67
Ethical criticism 9, 117–40

Feidelson, Charles 52
Formalism, *see* New Criticism, American
French, Marilyn 73, 85
Friedman, Maurice 56, 59

Frye, Joanne 140
Frye, Northrop 4–5, 38, 88, 123, 125–34

Gadamer, Hans-Georg 21
Gelpi, Albert 9
Gilkey, Langdon 45, 46
Goldberg, S. L. 68, 70
Gunn, Giles B. 5, 8, 10, 29–30, 37, 46, 70, 118, 121, 137

Hamilton, William 56
Hartman, Geoffrey 87
Harvey, W. J. 18
Hayman, David 71, 72
Hermeneutics 4, 6, 87, 93, 114, 119, 137
Hesla, David 119
Hirsch, E. D. 21
Hoffman, Daniel 47
Hopper, Stanley Romaine 4, 37, 68, 69, 70, 121
Hoy, David, C. 20, 87, 137

Irony 97, 98–9, 106, 107–8
Irony, implicative 93, 107, 109–16
Iser, Wolfgang 135–40
Iser, Wolfgang 4, 5, 29, 72, 73, 85, 94, 99, 106, 107, 118, 121, 122

Jaffe, Aniela 33, 37
James, William 60
Jameson, Fredric 3, 87
Jasper, David 11
Jauss, Hans Robert 94, 137
Josipovici, Gabriel 123
Joyce, James 3, 7, 64–86
Jung, C. G. 11, 29–39

Kain, Richard 75
Kant 22, 26
Kaufman, S. Bruce 10
Kaul, A. N. 43
Kenner, Hugh 74

160

Index

Kenny, Alice 113
Kermode, Frank 44
Kort, Wesley 44, 124

Langbaum, Robert 65
Lanham, Jon 71
Lee, A. Robert 51
Lentricchia, Frank 18, 25, 130
Lewis, R. W. B. 40, 60
Literary criticism 11–19

Maddox, James 83, 85
Magliola, Robert 86, 113
Mailloux, Steven 138
Melville, Herman 3, 7, 40–63
Michaels, Walter Benn 135
Miller, David L. 38
Miller, J. Hillis 1, 8, 118, 119, 120, 137, 138–9
Murdoch, Iris 3–4, 6–7, 69, 72, 87–116

Nabokov, Vladimir 88
Natanson, Maurice 73
New Criticism, American 3, 10, 20, 31, 86, 92, 122, 124, 128, 129, 135

Palmer, Richard 114
Phenomenology 135

Plato 12
Poirier, Richard 135
Price, Martin 122

Reader-response criticism 2–3, 4, 29, 66, 87, 93, 108, 117–18, 120, 121, 135, 138
Religion and literature 1, 4, 5, 6, 7, 8, 9–10, 11, 18, 29–30, 36–7, 38, 92, 93, 117–18, 120, 121, 136, 138, 139
Ricoeur, Paul 120
Ross-Bryant, Lynn 38
Rossman, Charles 83

Said, Edward 3, 6, 91
Scholes, Robert 65, 66, 72, 88–9, 109
Scott, Nathan A., Jr 61, 70, 118, 121
Stevens, Wallace 120, 140
Structuralism 87, 88
Suleiman, Susan 137

Tanner, Tony 50, 59–60
Thomas, Brook 83–4
Toliver, Harold 111–12
Tompkins, Jane 135

Wheelwright, Philip 2, 20, 27, 38
Wimmers, Inge Crosman 9
Wimsatt, W. K. 129